Christmas 1965

DAVID W. NOBLE

HISTORIANS
against HISTORY

The Frontier Thesis and the
National Covenant in
American Historical Writing
since 1830

UNIVERSITY OF MINNESOTA PRESS
Minneapolis

Library of Congress Catalog Card Number: 65-22811

PUBLISHED IN GREAT BRITAIN, INDIA, AND PAKISTAN BY THE OXFORD
UNIVERSITY PRESS, LONDON, BOMBAY, AND KARACHI, AND IN CANADA BY
THE COPP CLARK PUBLISHING CO. LIMITED, TORONTO

FOR LOIS

PREFACE

I WOULD like to think that this book expresses a growing tradition among a community of scholars working in the history of ideas. My first interest in the history of historical thought came from the teaching of E. Harris Harbison and my reading in the writings of Carl Becker. I was further influenced by Herbert Butterfield's analysis of English historiography and Paul Farmer's research in French historiography. My concept of the American climate of opinion began to take shape at the end of the 1940's, influenced by the historians Eric Goldman, Stow Persons, Merle Curti, and Ralph Gabriel and by the literary students of American culture Leslie Fiedler, Lionel Trilling, and Henry Nash Smith.

Since 1950, I have learned much from a younger group of scholars, Richard Hofstadter, David Levin, Charles Sanford, Leo Marx, John Greene, John William Ward, Marvin Meyers, Henry May, Rush Welter, Loren Baritz, Robert Berkhofer, Jr., Cushing Strout, and many others. I thank them all for making this study possible. I have special thanks for my close friends in American cultural history, Arthur S. P. Berger, Hyman Berman, and Joseph Kwiat. I am very grateful to Jeanne Sinnen for her excellent editing of the manuscript. I cannot adequately express my debt to my wife whose help was absolutely indispensable to the accomplishment of this project.

D. W. N.

June 1965

TABLE OF CONTENTS

Historians against History

1 FLIGHT FROM FEUDALISM: THE NEW WORLD AND THE PURITAN COVENANT

IN THIS book, I have attempted to define the central tradition of American historical writing from 1830 to the present. It is my thesis that the point of view of the modern American historian is directly related to the world view of the English Puritans who came to Massachusetts. These Englishmen believed that the community they established in the New World was sustained by a covenant with God which delivered them and their children from the vicissitudes of history as long as they did not fail in their responsibility to keep their society pure and simple. The concept of a Biblical commonwealth was replaced in the eighteenth century by the Enlightenment's belief that the society of the English colonies rested on natural principles and that the new republic that emerged from the American Revolution had a covenant with nature which freed it from the burdens of European history as long as its citizens avoided the creation of complexity. When we meet our first great national historian, George Bancroft, in the 1830's, his interpretation of our past synthesizes the Biblical covenant of the Puritans and the natural covenant of Jefferson and asserts that this national covenant, which provides timeless harmony to the United States and separates Americans from the shifting patterns of European history, had found its final expression in Jacksonian democracy.

Bancroft identifies the crucial role the historian will play in our culture. Delineating the ahistorical uniqueness of America, he is the nation's chief political theorist. And just as the historian is the citizen who is most responsible for describing our covenant, he is also the one most responsible for defending it — he is our most important secular theologian. Like the

3

Puritan theologians of the second half of the seventeenth century, our historians have accepted the burden of warning the people when they stray from the purity and simplicity demanded to preserve the covenant. Since Bancroft, therefore, our great historians have been Jeremiahs; they have written Jeremiads as they have described the appearance of alien complexity in the nation which could bring Americans back within the transitory patterns of European history.

This is the tragic message of Frederick Jackson Turner who in 1890 had to declare that the importation of industrialism from Europe had destroyed the physical frontier which Bancroft had argued was the foundation of our national covenant. But in the next generation, Charles Beard was to offer the hope that the new complexity of the nineteenth century was not the result of Old World industrialism but was rather caused by the intrusion of other, more artificial, European traditions and institutions. This was a hopeful message because Beard then asserted that industrialism was a natural force which could destroy this artificial European culture and restore the natural covenant characterized by the pristine restraint of Jefferson's republic.

By 1945, however, it no longer seemed possible that the vast institutional edifice of corporations and governmental bureaucracy could vanish. If the tradition of the Puritan covenant, which had declared the New World beyond the influence of European historical patterns, was to be preserved, it must be redefined so that this institutional complexity could be incorporated within the covenant with nature. This has been the task of our most recent generation of historians, who are represented in this book by Daniel Boorstin.

This is the major theme to be unfolded in the following pages. The American people believe that their historical experience has been uniquely timeless and harmonious because they are the descendants of Puritans who, in rejecting the traditions and institutions of the Old World, promised never to establish traditions and institutions in the New World. If history is the record of changing institutions and traditions, then by definition there can be no history in a nation which by puritanical resolve refuses to create complexity. And the American historian is the chief spokesman for this cultural tradition. From 1830 to the present, each generation has seen the emergence of a historian who has become a public philosopher as he differentiates between the timeless harmony of the real America and the intrusion of artificial and alien patterns from abroad. It is the supreme irony of our national culture and of our historical writing that, in the name of American uniqueness and separation from European civilization, we are preserving in the 1960's the traditions of the first Englishmen who came to establish a New England.

The English Puritans were converts to the Calvinist theology which rejected the authority of the central institution of medieval civilization, the Roman Catholic Church. For the Puritan, the most important relationship for the individual is that with God; it must be direct and personal. One does not find God or God's truth in the teachings of an earthly institution like the Church. The Church, as an institution, is temporal. Its position changes through history. It cannot possess the eternal immutability of God's word. The everlasting and unchanging word of God the Puritans found only in the Bible. To achieve salvation and to serve God in this world, it was necessary then for the Puritan to step out of the history of Catholic Europe and return to the timelessness of the primitive Christian church that existed before the development of the Roman Catholic Church. History, for the Puritans, was the sinful record of the institutional structure of the Roman Church and its traditions. When one rejected the authority of the Church, one rejected the authority of the past.

In Puritan theology it was assumed that God made a covenant of works with Adam which promised Adam a perfect life on earth as long as he kept God's law. But Adam sinned, the covenant was broken, and all Adam's seed, all future mankind, was to be punished for this failure to keep the covenant. The Puritans also assumed, however, that God had made a second covenant with man, the covenant of grace. Merciful God had decided to provide salvation to undeserving man if he would but have faith.

The Puritans further assumed that when God gave of His grace freely to an individual, that individual would be able to discover God's fundamental truths and laws in the world for the first time. When Adam fell, he had lost his capacity to reason. Man afterward had lived by the misleading forces of imagination, passion, and will, compounding their sinfulness. Now, however, God in His infinite mercy had given grace to a number of Englishmen who became Puritans as they learned of the necessity of abandoning medieval civilization and of beginning a new society based on God's truth as revealed to their clarified reason. For the English Puritans, the basic core of this new revelation was that God wanted man to live in a simple relationship with Him. God wanted men to form autonomous congregations as the basic theological and social unit for the purpose of worshipping Him. The voluntary association of the congregation must replace the complex hierarchy of the Roman Catholic Church and the continued complexity of the existing Anglican Church.

But for the English Puritan living through the turbulent decade of the 1620's, there was the inescapable question of how purification and simplification could take place. The leaders of the English Church were against them, the king was against them. Help for their position might come from Parliament but the king refused to govern with the help of that body. How was England to be purified, how was the corruption of history to be swept away to achieve the simplicity that was God's will?

In the 1620's, there seemed to be no real hope that a revolution could sweep away the poisoned past. The saints were too few, their enemies were too many and too powerful. But a dedicated band of Puritans might leave England and go to North America, there to form a New England. Here their children might grow without the baleful influence of sinful England. They were not deserting England, however; they were leaving the old island in order to ensure her salvation. They were the saving remnant of England; they had the responsibility of regenerating all England. The only way to accomplish this awful task at the moment was to withdraw to the empty lands across the sea and there to establish the model of what God wanted Old England to become. The community of saints in New England would teach men by example what they could and should do; they would restore the supremacy of God's word in the world.

For those Puritans who left Old England, there was then a strong sense of representing the English nation. And they now added to their theological relationship with God the idea of a national covenant. God expected man to live in a national community; He expected man to work to redeem this national community. And God was willing to covenant with the men of a national community. The terms of this contract would be God's promise to give permanent life to the nation if its members kept God's laws. Human history, in the Puritan outlook, was marked by the ceaseless rise and decline of social groups because sinful man was not capable of building a truly good society. Now God had given this New World nation the chance to escape the rhythm that had marked all previous nations. This was a community of saints. For the first time since the rise of the Roman Catholic Church had destroyed the primitive church, a society based on God's laws existed. This was God's nation and He would preserve it as long as its members resisted the corrupting influences which still existed in the Old World.

In a nation outside of history, the purpose of theology was no longer to justify revolution; it was rather to conserve the *status quo*. Puritan theologians became historians who explained how historical change had culminated in Massachusetts with the national covenant. The great theological problem, the great moral problem, the great historical problem became the preservation of the covenant. If the people moved away from the existing order, they would break the national covenant with God and be plunged back into the perils of history. Puritan theologians as historians promised their people that they could have economic progress without losing the covenant; but the people were not to create new traditions or institutions nor were they to accept old English traditions and institutions. They must retain the existing theological purity and social simplicity.

The Puritan of Massachusetts Bay cannot be made into the typical American. It is nevertheless clear that the Puritans began a tradition which entered most powerfully into the imagination of the United States when the new nation took shape in the late eighteenth century. In the days of the founding fathers, New England formed America's most closely knit cultural region, the one with the richest intellectual and educational resources. But beyond this direct impact of Puritanism on the intellectual history of our country, one must be aware of another influence of the Puritan outlook on America. This came by way of the Enlightenment, a secularized form of Puritanism that invaded the European continent during the eighteenth century and then crossed the ocean to the New World.

An English Puritan sympathizer, John Locke, was the architect of the theoretical cornerstone for the Enlightenment. This was the idea of nature as the basis of political community. In the 1620's when the New England Puritans had left their homeland to found a community based on a covenant with God, they expected their example to show the way for Old England; revolution did occur in England but by 1660 Puritan attempts to create a Biblical commonwealth there had been decisively defeated. It was clear that there was not sufficient consensus among the various Protestant groups to use religious revelation as the principle of political organization and action. When James II threatened Parliament's hard-won power in the 1680's, and its leaders sought grounds for effective opposition to the crown, a new political theory was needed that would unite the community around a secular position. Locke provided it.

To achieve political purity, according to Locke, men must look backward, beyond the beginning of civilization, to find the eternal truths on which to build the good society. Locke asserted that the first men had lived in a timeless state of nature. Here they had all the necessary political rights, the inalienable rights of life, liberty, and property. Here also men had the necessary political virtue of reason. Since some men, however, did not operate under the guidance of reason, a political community was necessary to restrain the wrongdoer and to protect the virtuous individual in his rights. This political community derived its authority from the individuals it represented and the government was, therefore, under constitutional restraint so that it could neither legally nor morally take from the individual his inalienable rights. If government did violate its authority, then the individual was justified in revolution against what had become tyranny.

The persuasive force of Locke's argument rested upon the prestige of the new natural science, which challenged the authority of the Aristotelian tradition of science, the official scientific position of the Roman Catholic Church and of medieval civilization. Isaac Newton was the greatest spokesman for the new science, and with his explanation for the orderliness of planetary relations in the solar system by the law of gravity, intelligent men became convinced that the medieval world view must be replaced by the concept of the Newtonian world machine. Now all enlightened men knew that nature was a unified whole, constructed from a common material substance, governed by uniform laws. Harmony for man, identical to nature's harmony, was possible if he lived by reason and not by his cultural inheritance of demonstrably false and irrational traditions preserved by equally irrational institutions. Harmony was possible for man if he stepped out of history to live by natural law.

Locke provided a psychological theory to prove that man was able to understand the laws of nature. If men had not seen clearly in the past, it was not because they could never see clearly; rather it was because they were taught to see the wrong things. Again it was historical accumulation, false traditions preserved in useless institutions, which had blinded men to the truth of nature. For Locke, the individual came into the world with a plastic mind, able to learn from his environment. All that a man is, is the result of his experience. If a society could be constructed along the lines of natural law, then men would experience only that which is good. Then the good and natural society would truly exist.

In England, however, the good society on behalf of which Locke developed his philosophical arguments was that of the tight-knit middle-class aristocracy of powerful merchants and landowners who controlled Parliament — and wanted to remain in control. The state of nature which they defended against the tyranny of James II was one of special privilege for a small minority of Englishmen. These men were free from the medieval past and for them this freedom was enough for the whole community. It was to be Frenchmen who, inspired by the secularization of English Puritanism by Locke and Newton, would take up the task of destroying medieval civilization, of bringing purity and simplicity and rationality to Europe, of bringing Enlightenment to replace the Dark Ages.

Assuming the self-evident truths of Locke's natural law as demonstrated in the theoretical structure of the Newtonian world machine, the French intellectuals began the attack on the vestiges of medieval civilization in their country by appealing to reason and the empirical method of scientific investigation. Reason understood that the model of the physical structure of the universe as revealed by Newton was one of simplicity and harmony; reason understood, therefore, that society must be simple and harmonious. But France was a nation filled with an irrational legal and political and social and economic structure. Everywhere there was special privilege which rested only on the authority of tradition which sprang from historical accident. When men questioned the irrational institutional structure of the day, however, they were told by the spokesmen of the established order that the historical medieval structure was sanctioned by tradition and by the authority of God's revelation. The French *philosophes* countered that medieval civilization represented the vagaries of misguided human imagination which changed over time, that the medieval outlook was not built on a rock of unchanging truth but on the inevitably transitory institutions of history. One could not demonstrate the validity of France's medieval culture by the methods of scientific investigation. It was, therefore, invalid. Rational men now refused to live by imaginations distorted by historical accumulations of myth. They lived only by scientifically instructed intelligence.

While the Puritan religious faith had become secularized and transformed into a vision of a harmonious natural order understandable to human reason, one should not underestimate its power to inspire its apparently agnostic adherents with an apocalyptic vision of a purified millennium that was to appear when the corrupt medieval past was burned away. These men were able to use the cutting edge of empirical science to destroy the value system of medieval civilization because they had faith that when this vast accumulation of false historical tradition was swept away, mankind would be able to see with a clarified reason the permanent values implicit in nature's laws upon which a new and better civilization could be erected. They were, further, certain that the existence of natural man amidst the confusions of history could be demonstrated. Each man, they believed, had natural characteristics; he was innately good and rational. These natural traits could not be altered or lost but they could be obscured. There was a superficial aspect of human nature that was shaped by the historical society of which the individual was a part. History was the record of these changing styles and patterns of the superficial side of humanity. The proper study of history was to cut through the record of the changing qualities of mankind and find the universal man, the man who represented the eternal verities and values of nature. The French Enlightenment historians shared the belief of their great English contemporary, Hume, that "Mankind are so much the same, in all times and places, that history informs us of nothing new or strange in this particular. Its chief use is only to discover the constant and universal principles of human nature." [1]

By 1749, the French *philosophes* were being presented with a new political theory to fit this new history, one articulated by Jean Jacques Rousseau. For Rousseau, when men returned to their original and natural condition, there would exist a new political community of the "people." The "people" would be free and equal individuals in a classless, institutionless, traditionless society, living in harmony with nature. The "people" would be sovereign, the source of all political authority, the source of all law. The "people" would act together in spontaneous unanimity through the agency of the General Will, the symbolic representation of the social unity formed by natural man's free act of association. No complexity, no corruption would be allowed to creep into the purified and simplified political life of the "people."

The partial acceptance of Rousseau by the *philosophes* dramatized the existence of a major paradox in the Enlightenment outlook. The French thinkers believed in progress. They believed that when men stepped out of medieval history to return to primitive simplicity and harmony, their minds would be freed to reason clearly and there would be a great advance in scientific knowledge. The *philosophes*, in the original Puritan pattern, believed that scientific knowledge must have practical application. It must

be used to build a better economy, a better way of life. When men escaped
the Dark Ages, cities would grow, learning would increase, the arts would
develop. A return to primitivism was to make possible a new, a better and
more complex civilization. But for Rousseau, the return to the "noble savage," the reachievement of ancient purity, meant the supremacy of the
heart over the head. Man's natural goodness, he argued, was to be found
in his instincts, not in his reasoning power. Intelligence, scientific learning,
the arts, were expressions of civilization. Civilization had corrupted the
natural man, had led him away from the purity of nature, and had taught
him the vices of historical society. Human salvation could only be achieved
in the return to primitive simplicity, and this meant a ruthless destruction
of the ways of civilization, including the arts and the sciences. The majority
of French intellectuals, however, refused to find such an absolute conflict
between their belief in the progress of civilization and their belief in a
purified and primitive state of nature. They continued to believe in both
progress and primitivism.

It was within this intellectual climate of opinion that the *philosophes*
discovered the existence of the British colonies in North America. At the
moment when they postulated with Voltaire the possibility of a new society built on the principles of political liberty and religious toleration, of
humanitarianism and enlightenment, they discovered the existence of just
such a society in America. At the moment when they postulated with Rousseau the possibility of a simple and happy society of noble savages living
with hearts purified by contact with physical nature, they discovered the
existence of just such a society in America, a society embodying the return to primitivism. At the moment when they were searching through history for the natural man, they found him in British North America.

When Benjamin Franklin arrived in France to explain the opposition
of the American colonies to the British restrictions on colonial economic
life, he was accepted by the *philosophes* as the symbolic representative of
both the progressive enlightenment of civilization and the simple purity
of primitive life. These men accepted Franklin as the great physical scientist of the Western world for his experiments in electricity. He was Voltaire's perfect philosopher: a rationalist, a scientist, a humanitarian. But
Franklin also represented the simplicity and goodness of heart which Rousseau demanded from his heroes.

Writing of Franklin and his America, the man and the country which
had escaped from the history of Europe, which had escaped from medi-

eval civilization, which had escaped from traditions and institutional complexity to live with nature, Frenchmen alternately saw America as the capital of a future progressive, scientific civilization and as the primitive and purified antithesis to civilization. Thinking of America as the maker of Franklin, the scientist and humanitarian, Raynal wrote that "Perhaps there will arise another Newton in New England. It is in British America, let there be no doubt on this, that the first rays of knowledge are to shine, if they are at last to dawn under this long obscured sky." [2] But the vision of Rousseau inspired Gaspard de Beaurieu to dedicate his book, *Élève de la nature*, to the Americans. "In that land which you inhabit and which you cultivate, there are to be found neither cities nor luxury nor crimes nor infirmities. Every day of your lives is serene, for the purity of your souls is communicated to the skies above you. You are free, you labor, and bring forth all about you, besides your abundant crops, a harvest of all the virtues. You are as Nature would wish us all to be. I therefore dedicate to you this portrait of a man whom I have conceived as formed by nature alone." [3]

When the American Revolution began, it became clear that here, across the Atlantic, European men were cutting all ties with that history which connected them with the medieval past. This was no revolution merely for the political independence of the English colonies: it was a revolution against the past, it was a revolution for the creation of the Enlightenment. For Louis Mercier in 1778, it was perhaps in "America that the human race is to be recreated; that it is to adopt a new and sublime legislation, that it is to perfect the arts and sciences." [4] Independent America in the eyes of the first great theorist of the idea of progress, Condorcet, demonstrated that men could step out of history with security, a new society could be built on natural laws. The great contribution of the newly formed United States of America to Europe, Condorcet wrote, was the living proof of the existence of the self-evident truths which previously could only be postulated by French thinkers. Turgot's prophecy about the Americans, that "They are the hope of the human race; they may well become its model," [5] was being fulfilled.

When Benjamin Franklin died in 1790, his place as the chief American representative of the Enlightenment was taken by Thomas Jefferson. Jefferson, too, had spent much time in France in close intellectual communication with the *philosophes*. And he too shared their view of America as the place where European aspirations achieved concrete expression, as the place where the ideal had become real. Jefferson accepted the view of the Physiocrats, the French *philosophes* who specialized in economic theory, that agricultural production was the basis of national prosperity. He was committed to the idea of Rousseau that a nation of simple farmers living in redemptive contact with the soil would naturally be virtuous. He shared with Condorcet the belief that the American Revolution had ushered in a new period of political reform and enlightenment. He carried on the tradition of Voltaire that in America there was a unique intellectual climate of tolerance, liberty, and humanitarianism. With the *philosophes*, he interpreted the constitutional conventions of the revolutionary states as a great contribution to the political problem of how the sovereignty of the people was to be established.

Ironically, however, the success of the American Revolution in separating America from feudal Europe had also separated Jefferson from the *philosophes*. For Jefferson, his European friends must continue to be philosophers, living in a world of theory which they opposed to the world of history. The intellectual discovery of the laws of nature told men they must escape from history to live with nature. But Europeans did not have a virgin land where men could fulfill the ideals of simplicity and equality, of reasonableness and purity. Only in America could one find this blessed state that made possible republican virtue. So Jefferson must write of the separation of America from Europe: "For this whole chapter in the history of man is new. . . . Before the establishment of the American States, nothing was known to history but the man of the old world, crowded within limits either small or overcharged, and steeped in the vices which that situation generates. A government adapted to such men would be one thing; but a very different one, that for the man of these States. Here every one may have land to labor for himself. . . . Every one, by his property . . . is interested in the support of law and order. And such men may safely and advantageously reserve to themselves a wholesome control over their public affairs, and a degree of freedom, which, in the hands of the *canaille* of the cities of Europe, would be instantly perverted to the demolition and destruction of everything public and private." [6]

Jefferson was now returning to the imagination of those Puritans who had left Old England to create a New England which would provide a model for European imitation. In order to establish this model, made possible by unspoiled nature, America must be kept free from European contamination, the contamination of history. Sounding more and more like a Puritan prophet, Jefferson wrote, "I . . . bless the Almighty Being, who, in gathering together the waters under the heavens into one place, divided the dry land of your hemisphere from the dry lands of ours, and said, at least be there peace. I hope that . . . its prosperity under the Charter will react on the mind of Europe, and profit her by the example." [7] Now he advised American youth against European travel, warning against the snare of European vices. Now he advised Americans to think of restricting immigration so that the natural purity of the American population would not be lost under the impact of the historically corrupt European.

The original Puritan emphasis on an elect, a chosen people with a national covenant from God, filled Jefferson's first inaugural address where he spoke as the spiritual shepherd of his flock. America, he announced, was "kindly separated by nature and a wide ocean from the exterminating havoc of one quarter of the globe; too high-minded to endure the degradations of the others; possessing a chosen country, with room enough for our descendents to the hundreth and thousandth generation; entertaining a due sense of our equal right to the use of our own faculties, to the acquisition of our industry, to honor and confidence from our fellow citizens, resulting not from birth but from our actions and their sense of them; enlightened by a benign religion, professed, indeed, and practiced in various forms, yet all of them including honesty, truth, temperance, gratitude, and the love of man; acknowledging and adoring an overruling Providence, which by all its dispensations proves that it delights in the happiness of man here and his greater happiness hereafter." [8]

The idea of the national covenant as it expressed itself in Jefferson's thought centered on the preservation of natural simplicity. The task of Americans, in Jefferson's mind, was to develop a way of life in harmony with nature. No institutional complexity must be allowed to develop, no infiltration of European tradition was to be permitted. For Jefferson, the Enlightenment definition of progress had reached total and final fulfillment in the America of 1800.

But just as the definition of America as a frontier for the fulfillment of English Puritanism had given way to the definition of America as the frontier for the fulfillment of the eighteenth-century Enlightenment, so the development of romanticism and democratic thought in Europe after 1776 called forth a new European definition of the American frontier as the fulfillment of another concept of progress. Taking inspiration from Rousseau's primitivism, new prophets of progress rejected the rational emphasis of the Enlightenment. Romantic poets cried out that man could not achieve organic harmony with nature through the abstract tool of reason. Reason separated man and nature. Only intuition, the reason of the heart, was capable of lifting man out of the artificial traditions of history and delivering him unto nature.

The *philosophes* had sinned still further in their emphasis on reason because they had created a philosophical justification for a new kind of aristocracy. All men were not equally endowed with reason. Some men understood natural laws better than others and, therefore, must provide leadership for their inferiors. There could never exist an order of equally free individuals, a democracy, until it was accepted that all individuals had equal ability to understand and live by the precepts of nature because each individual was endowed equally with intuition. Romanticism and democracy must replace rationalism and republicanism before the artificial complexities of historical culture were transcended and progress reached its culmination in mankind's organic harmony with nature.

Americans were swept up in this latest definition of the final stage of progress. Between 1776 and 1828, they increasingly rejected the emphasis the founding fathers had placed on reason; they rejected the Federalist fear of democracy and majority rule. With greater and greater enthusiasm, they accepted the ideas of will and intuition, of democracy and the general will. And they became self-conscious converts to the Enlightenment theory of history as progress. But the American romantic democrats, like their European contemporaries, proclaimed that the *philosophes* had not really understood the idea of progress.

The thinkers of the eighteenth century, it was argued, conceived progress in mechanical terms as a sudden and dramatic step out of meaningless history into nature made possible by the use of reason. For the new romantics, however, progress was a historical process. Throughout the centuries, one could perceive a sequence of stages of civilization each morally better than the preceding one. This upward surge was designed to liberate the individual from the corruption of past civilizations and to place him in harmony with the spiritual presence of God in nature. The men of the Enlightenment were wrong, therefore, when they believed that men could consciously choose to end history; they were wrong when they believed that reason would unite man with God and nature. Men must wait for the process of progress to deliver them out of complexity into simplicity and they must achieve organic harmony through intuition and imagination. The romantic prophets of progress agreed with the rationalists of the Enlightenment that primitivism was the final goal of progress; but they argued that man must wait humbly and patiently for the course of historical development to reach this point. For American romantics this moment was to occur about 1830.

When Americans today affirm that they have no history because the United States is in harmony with nature, they do not define the national experience in the terms of seventeenth-century Puritanism or the eighteenth-century Enlightenment. They do so with the concepts of early nineteenth-century romanticism and democracy. We have had a constant self-definition as a nation from the 1830's to the present. Our final vision of the frontier is that which came from the Europe of Rousseau and Hegel.

If, for the American imagination, progress reached final fulfillment in the United States of 1830, if after the election of Andrew Jackson, the American people believed that change could no longer take place because all the vestiges of the European past had been swept away, then modern American historians have had a peculiar intellectual and moral burden. It is the historian as theologian and political theorist who explains how Americans have come to be a chosen people living under the protection of a national covenant with God and nature and who must defend that covenant from corruption.

The Jeremiads written by these historians tend toward the expression of a ritual drama. First there is the victory of progress over the medieval past. Here natural simplicity conquers historical complexity until American innocence is safely established within the sheltering arms of benevolent nature. The reality of an eternal, immutable ideal has defeated the artificiality of ephemeral, materialistic institutions and traditions. This great progressive drama is then followed by a series of minor dramas in which the established ideal is challenged by alien forces and in which the people rally to defend the ark of the covenant.

From the Old World where progress had not yet triumphed comes the challenge of evil men, representing ancient institutions and traditions. These villains will endeavor to undermine American virtue; they will try to tempt the people back into historical complexity. But the historian, as guardian of the national covenant, will illuminate these alien influences. The historian will demonstrate that which is real and American and that which is artificial and alien. The people, sure of this distinction, will then reject the Old World influence and rededicate themselves to the preservation of the New World Eden.

Such minor dramas must perpetually reoccur as long as the Old World remains in the clutches of historical complexity. And as long as the metaphysical distinction between European history and American nature remains, the American historian will carry the responsibility of being the chief theologian and political theorist of his nation. He must always explain how his country has achieved its uniqueness and he must always warn against the intrusion of alien influence.

This is the historical and philosophical background we need to have if we are to understand the writings of George Bancroft, the historian of Jacksonian democracy, the first modern historian who assumed the burden of being the political theorist and theologian of his generation, the first modern historian whose writings exemplify the qualities of the seventeenth-century Puritan Jeremiad modified by the influence of romanticism and democracy.

2 GEORGE BANCROFT: NATURE AND THE FULFILLMENT OF THE COVENANT

Our cultural historians in the twentieth century have written again and again that George Bancroft symbolizes the liberation of the nineteenth-century American imagination from bondage to the colonial past. Russel Nye, for example, in his analysis of the earlier historian lays emphasis on Bancroft's rejection of Puritan theology, which according to Nye linked New England to Europe until Bancroft's generation revolutionized New England by establishing Unitarianism as the dominant religious outlook.[1]

This traditional approach to Bancroft begins his biography with his minister father, Aaron, who had broken from five generations of orthodox commitment to Congregationalism in leading his flock toward the new heresy of Unitarianism. Born in 1800, George Bancroft was reared in a home full of intellectual ferment. As a child, he was encouraged to discuss and debate theological doctrine with his father and his father's friends. He was given the classics of world history to read. The youthful prodigy was led to see that Unitarianism was the logical culmination of history. He was then sent to Harvard which had become a center of liberal theology under the leadership of its new president, John Kirkland. This is the brief intellectual biography which so inexorably depicts George Bancroft as a rebel against conservative New England tradition.

When one begins to read Bancroft's histories, however, one discovers that the young New Englander considered himself a rebel against the philosophy of the Enlightenment, not the theology of Puritanism. Professor Nye describes an essay written by Bancroft at Harvard in praise of Jon-

18

athan Edwards as a momentary youthful rebellion against the Unitarian pressures of his home and the college, a momentary aberration from Bancroft's fundamental commitment to the Unitarian revolution. But in the philosophical writings of the mature Bancroft, one finds nothing but praise for Jonathan Edwards. He calls Edwards the first great philosophical idealist and the first great spokesman for the idea of progress. And Bancroft was thoroughly dedicated to the philosophy of idealism which was so critical of the materialism and mechanical rationalism of the Enlightenment.

It was in Germany after graduation from Harvard that Bancroft's point of view crystallized. There he studied with theologians, philosophers, and historians who were critics of the Enlightenment from the same perspective of philosophical idealism held by Jonathan Edwards. George Bancroft returned from Germany an enthusiastic romantic dedicated to history as the process of progress, a process to be intuited. He was now an enthusiastic democrat, arguing the equality of all men through the instinct of intuition and affirming the possibility of the expression of a general will through the mystical union of the individual's intuition in the organic unity of the people. The fulfillment of progress, Bancroft proclaimed, depended upon the disappearance of medieval civilization and the achievement of a state of nature. European nations must await the disestablishment of the institutions and traditions of the Dark Ages. But as for America, the reality of America was nature. The medieval past was never an integral part of the New World. And so, he was certain, the United States would arrive at the millennium before any other nation.

Bancroft began his explanation of American history, therefore, with a theological affirmation of the omnipotence of God. Calvin, he wrote in his *History of the United States,* was the greatest theologian of the modern world because of his insistence on predestination. For Bancroft, Calvin erred only in believing that man should worship this omnipotent God in a single churchly institution. Calvin did not understand that each man must be free to worship God in his own way. Bancroft was absolute in his defense of the individual's freedom from restraint by worldly institutions. He was also absolute in his defense of God's power to shape the destiny of the individual.

This is why Bancroft's theological and philosophical criticism was directed not against the Puritan tradition but against the Enlightenment, especially its French representatives. Here was mortal error which misled men and caused them to believe that, through the free use of their reason, they could discover natural law and conform to it. The French *philosophes* had cut man off from God, from humanity, from history, and from progress. The French had visualized self-sufficient individuals living in timeless harmony by a rational understanding of abstract natural law. Against French materialism, Bancroft contrasted a philosophy of idealism. It was the last great Puritan and first great philosophical idealist, Jonathan Edwards, who in the eighteenth century postulated a philosophy of progress which "was nobler than the theory of Vico: more grand and general than the method of Bossuet, it embraced in outline the whole 'work of redemption,' — the history of the influence of all moral truth in the gradual regeneration of humanity. The meek New England divine, in his quiet association with the innocence and simplicity of rural life, knew that in every succession of revolutions, the cause of civilization and moral reform is advanced. 'The new creation' — such are his words — 'is more excellent than the old. So it ever is, that when one thing is removed by God to make way for another, the new excels the old.' — 'The wheels of Providence,' he adds, 'are not turned about by blind chance, but they are full of eyes round about, and they are guided by the spirit of God. Where the spirit goes, they go.' Nothing appears more self-determined than the volitions of each individual; and nothing is more certain than that the providence of God will overrule them for good. The finite will of man, free in its individuality, is, in the aggregate, subordinate to general laws." [2]

In these sentences appears all that is fundamental to Bancroft's philosophy of history. Progress is the will of God; progress is the forward movement of redemption of humanity; progress is supported by some individuals, opposed by others, and transcends their support and opposition. Progress is the movement from complexity to simplicity; progress is the movement from ancient Europe to rural America. Progress is escape from the instability of history to the stability of nature.

Drawing upon the authority of Edwards and the modern German philosophers, Bancroft reiterated his belief in philosophical idealism. "The universe is the reflex and image of its Creator. . . . Harmony is the characteristic of the intellectual system of the universe; and immutable laws of moral existence must pervade all time and all space, all ages and all worlds. . . . shall we not believe that the type of all intellectual life likewise exists in the Divine mind." [3] And Bancroft used this technical philosophy of absolute spirituality to criticize the Enlightenment for making man a passive adherent to unchanging material laws of physical nature. How then was he to relate this philosophic idealism to the Jeffersonian covenant with nature, which owed so much to the Enlightenment view of physical nature as the foundation on which a new civilization was to be built?

Bancroft began this synthesis by demonstrating that a universe which expresses God is at once dynamic and static. If there is progress, then there must be change. If there is change, then the world must be dynamic. "Unceasing movement," he wrote, "is the law of whatever is infinite." [4] But Bancroft argued that this dynamic movement of God's spirit which man can see in the great drama of historical change over thousands of years did not represent a change in God or in God's plan for humanity.

Men, the children of God, have been given the opportunity to fulfill His will on earth. History as progress will commence when men begin to destroy those civilizations which they have made by their own will and out of their own imaginations. Progress is the escape of men from the evil and complex cultures they have built to the simplicity and purity of God's law. The immutable truths that men discover in the course of progress have always existed: "No science has been reached, no thought generated, no truth discovered, which has not from all time existed potentially in every human mind. . . . The necessity of the progress of the race follows, therefore, from the fact that the great Author of all life has left truth in its immutability to be observed, and has endowed man with the power of observation and generalization." [5] Evolution, history, progress meant the gradual revelation of God's plan to mankind and man's gradual adherence to this pre-established ideal. Bancroft had banished the static philosophy of the Enlightenment but he had made it possible for Americans to have a new stability. And ultimately he would lead his people back to the nature of the *philosophes,* a nature purified and spiritualized by theology.

Next Bancroft faced the problem of destroying the doctrine of reason held by the French thinkers while providing an adequate substitute, again properly purified and spiritualized. If the major intellectual problem for man was not that of adjusting to a static world of physical nature but rather of communicating with the dynamic spirit of God, then necessarily "We have not merely the senses opening to us the external world, but an internal sense, which places us in connexion with the world of intelligence and the decrees of God." [6] In the tradition of American transcendentalism, Bancroft chose to call this "higher faculty" reason; the reason of the Enlightenment would be demoted to a mundane level of understanding.

Bancroft now had prepared the philosophical foundations for assuring his generation that it was out of history, that it had achieved permanent harmony as a chosen people protected by a covenant with God from the perils that pursued the rest of mankind. He had prepared the philosophical foundation for meeting all charges that Jacksonian democracy was an alien concept bent on the overthrow of the civilization of the founding fathers. For him, the essential fact of America in the 1830's was Jacksonian democracy. The basic belief of this new democracy was that the people, the majority of the common men, must govern. Many critics from the New England aristocracy assailed this faith, arguing that the people would destroy all the virtue, all the values of traditional civilization. Prophets of despair and doom argued that the idea of democracy was the vulgar, leveling, atheistic ideology of the French Revolution let loose in America. But wait before judging, demanded Bancroft of the New England gentlemen. Those who damn democracy as alien and atheistic are utterly mistaken. Democracy is pure Christianity, it is the will of God, it is the culmination of spiritual progress, it is implicit in the state of nature which is the real America.

Democracy, he wrote, is the complete freedom of each individual from earthly restraint. Now it follows, Bancroft argued, that if in a democracy all individuals are equally free from the distorting influence of traditions and institutions, then they are necessarily free to use their intuition, their reason, to find God's will and God's law and to obey that will and law. When all the individuals in a community followed God's way, they were all purified and then they became the voice of God. This was the basis of that new political phenomenon, the people: "If it be true, that the gifts of mind and heart are universally diffused, if the sentiment of truth, justice, love, and beauty exists in everyone, then it follows . . . that the common judgment in taste, politics, and religion is the highest authority on earth, and the nearest possible approach to an infallible decision." [7] And for Bancroft, such democracy existed in an America that was the complete antithesis of medieval civilization. Here all men were free because they had become the children of nature. Rejoice, wrote Bancroft, because "The absence of the prejudices of the old world leaves us here opportunity of consulting independent truth; and man is left to apply the instinct of freedom to every social relation and public interest. We have approached so near to nature, that we can hear her gentlest whispers; we have made Humanity our law giver and our oracle; and, therefore, the nation receives, vivifies, and applies principles, which in Europe the wisest accept with distrust. Freedom of mind and . . . each great truth is firmly grasped, comprehended and enforced. . . . the spirit of God breathes through the combined intelligence of the people." [8]

Bancroft's histories were a justification of the democratic revolution that had destroyed the pattern of politics of the founding fathers, which had concentrated political leadership in the hands of a few important families. He was justifying a fundamental change in the nation between the presidency of Jefferson and that of Jackson. He was apparently questioning the timeless perfection of the Jeffersonian covenant with nature. His strategy, however, was to deny that Jacksonian democracy was a revolution. Instead, he argued that the election of Jackson symbolized the triumphant defense of the Jeffersonian covenant against the attack of an un-American aristocracy.

Bancroft's conservative argument began with his thesis that European man, fettered by the established institutional structure in the Old World, became free as soon as he set foot on the American shore. He and his equally free comrades immediately became part of the democratic community of the people. From the beginning of American history, therefore, Bancroft insisted, the people, free and equal and independent, have always formed the basis of the American nation. Logically, there could not be a Jacksonian "revolution" to overthrow a colonial aristocracy and "establish" the rule of the people. The American nation as Jacksonian democracy existed as soon as the first Europeans settled within the sheltering arms of nature: "The elements of our country, such as she exists today, were already there. Of the institutions of the Old World, monarchy had no motive to emigrate. . . . The feudal aristocracy had accomplished its mission in Europe; it could gain no new life . . . [in] the wilderness. . . . Priestcraft did not emigrate . . . to the forests of America. . . . Nothing came from Europe but a free people. The people, separating itself from all other elements of previous civilization; the people, self-confiding and industrious; the people, wise by all traditions that favored popular happiness — the people alone broke away from European influence, and in the New World laid the foundations of our republic. . . . The people alone were present in power. Like Moses, they had escaped from Egyptian bondage to the wilderness, that God might there give them the pattern of the tabernacle." [9]

The people, the expression of God's will, were, like that will, a timeless absolute. There was no history of the people in America between 1600 and 1830. There could be no history of the people because they lived by the unchanging will of God and in the unchanging environment of nature, and not in the changing texture of human culture.

In philosophical triumph, Bancroft turned on those who attacked the Jacksonians as revolutionists who were building democracy on the basis of foreign and atheistic ideology. Behold, he declared, the natural democracy which existed in every English colony from the moment of its organization. Look, he demanded, at Virginia which immediately "established upon her soil the supremacy of the popular branch, the freedom of trade, the independence of religious societies, the security from foreign taxation, and the universal elective franchise. . . . Virginia had herself, almost unconsciously, established a nearly independent democracy." [10] Look also, he continued, at Maryland, which "like Virginia . . . [was] in full possession of liberty, based upon the practical assertion of the sovereignty of the people. Like Virginia, it had so nearly completed its constitution, that, till the epoch of its final separation from England, it hardly made any further advance towards freedom and independence." [11] Even of Massachusetts, he claimed, "The trading corporation was unconsciously become a republican democracy." And he grew rhapsodic when he described the first commonwealth carved from the inland frontier, Connecticut: "The constitution which was thus framed was of unexampled liberality. . . . Nearly two centuries have elapsed . . . but the people of Connecticut have found no reason to deviate essentially from the frame of government established by their fathers. . . . the laws of honest justice were the basis of their commonwealth; and therefore its foundations were lasting. These humble emigrants invented an admirable system; for they were very near to Nature, listened willingly to her voice, and easily copied her forms." [12]

No, thundered Bancroft, there was no history of the people; there was no Jacksonian revolution; there was no recent emergence of democracy in America. And he proceeded to write ten volumes to prove this point.

In spite of the fact that apparently all the drama of history as progress had ended for Americans in 1600, Bancroft still found the ingredients of a great historical drama that stretched from Jamestown in 1607 to Yorktown in 1781. After all, the New World was still tied to the Old. The reactionary and degenerate forces of Catholicism continued to surround the Americans on the north and south. And the Americans were still part of the British Empire; they still payed homage to a king. The full meaning of their democratic experience could not become clear until the Old World forces of Catholicism and monarchy were driven from the Western hemisphere. The natural democracy of the early seventeenth-century colonies must become totally independent of European history.

Bancroft, who described the natural democrats in terms of perfect Christlike innocence, made it clear that the Americans were not able to destroy these Old World influences. To engage in political and martial warfare would rob the American of his perfect innocence. Having escaped from the disharmony of history to the harmony of God's nature, the American must not lose that spiritual perfection by re-entering history to engage in conflict. It was England, therefore, inspired by Protestant truth (for the Anglo-Saxons of England had gone furthest of all the European nations in throwing off the past) but still caught up in the spiritual compromise of historical experience, which must act as God's agency to liberate the Americans from European influence. The drama of American history between 1600 and 1776 then, for Bancroft, was the destruction of medieval history in the New World by England.

As England entered the seventeenth century, he wrote, one might see the vast stirrings of God's liberal truth. By 1600, the Tudors had smashed the power of the Roman Catholic Church and the feudal aristocracy. This monarchy had served God's purpose but now it had in turn become reactionary and must be destroyed. And one could see in the Puritan independents the model of the democratic people who would populate the English colonies. These men had the vision of the perfect commonwealth of free and equal individuals. They struggled to destroy all ancient privilege in England, they struggled to sweep away the vast accumulation of history which lay so heavy on the land, and they failed. In England, unlike the English colonies, there were aristocrats and peasants. These men were not fired by the Protestant ideal of an equal and independent citizenry. They blocked the efforts of the middle-class independents to create liberty and equality.

When the Puritan revolution failed and a Stuart king was restored to the throne, the march of progress was threatened in America as well as in England. The Stuarts planned to destroy the liberty of the English colonies. But the very reactionary nature of the doctrine of divine-right monarchy led to the destruction of the Stuarts. Following the logic of reaction, James II came to espouse the ultimate of reactionary philosophy, the Church of Rome. This reversion to the medieval past aroused the antagonism of the merchant aristocracy which had embraced Protestantism but which had refused to accept the idea of democracy. This group had refused to help the Independents during the 1640's in their battle to destroy medieval political institutions. Now, however, this class had no choice but to destroy the medieval monarchy in order to preserve its Protestantism. The commercial aristocracy unwillingly became the agent of progress and established the new political theory of the supremacy of Parliament. But Bancroft made it clear that England had not become a democracy. Parliament was absolutely controlled by this new aristocracy.

Bancroft briefly contrasted this undemocratic and class-directed revolution in England, the so-called Glorious Revolution of 1688, with the truly democratic revolution in America where the people arose spontaneously without leadership to defend their rights against Stuart tyranny. "Thus did a popular insurrection, beginning at Boston, extend to the Chesapeake, and to the wilderness," an insurrection that " 'made a great noise in the world.' Its object was Protestant liberty." [13]

The Americans in their freedom and innocence did not immediately realize that the revolution in England had not established liberty for all. They did not understand that the commercial aristocracy also detested the democracy of the North American colonies. They did not foresee that this class, through its control of the institution of Parliament, would ultimately attack the liberty of the colonials. But before the reactionary nature of the merchant aristocracy was to reveal itself, it still had the progressive mission of making the New World safe for democracy by destroying the political power of Catholicism. The dynamic commercial leaders of England were carried by their greed and selfishness into conflict with the imperial interests of Spain and France. Seeking aid on the continent against these powerful foes, Protestant Englishmen naturally allied with Protestant Prussia.

Gradually, Bancroft brought his reader through the tortuous passages of European diplomacy and war toward one of the great turning points in human history. When the Protestant and Catholic powers locked in mortal combat at the middle of the eighteenth century in the Seven Years War, nothing less was at stake than this epic issue: "Shall the Reformation developed to the fulness of free inquiry, succeed in its protest against the

Middle Age?" [14] But how could the vigor of Protestant individualism fail to destroy the degenerate Catholics who had not God but only decadent Rome for an ally?

By 1760, the Roman Church, represented by France and Spain, was smashed by the forces of progress — the Protestant monarchies England and Prussia. But these Protestant countries, still ruled by kings and privileged classes, were able to play no further role in the pageant of God's progress. All they could accomplish was the destruction of Catholicism; this they had done. Now after 1760, the seeds of Protestant individualism were planted in the Catholic monarchies. Hopefully, they might grow and lead the people toward emancipation from feudal history. In France, for instance, there were now to appear philosophers of individualism, nature, and democracy like Turgot and Rousseau. Here, in the nation which was soon to become the friend of the American Revolution, "Individuality was the groundwork of new theories in politics, ethics, and industry." [15]

But the monarch and the privileged class of Protestant England, now freed from the epic struggle with Catholicism, turned to destroy the democracy of the English colonies. This reactionary political movement in England was still part of God's plan of progress. Although God's American children, having reached a state of innocence and perfect virtue, could not initiate aggressive action to separate themselves from semifeudal England, this step had to be taken because the world must be shown that God's design for mankind had not culminated in England or Prussia. Democracy was the final stage of God's kingdom on earth and democracy existed only in the English colonies. This perfection must be revealed to mankind.

How fortunate and how necessary for God's design then that England should have in 1760 a George III and a merchant aristocracy who would work together to attempt to destroy American liberties! How fortunate and necessary it was that the American democrats, in order to defend these liberties, must declare their independence from England and proclaim to the Old World the existence of the perfect democratic society and government in the New World!

A sophisticated historian who worked from the original sources, Bancroft knew that the conflict of the British crown and Parliament against the American colonies was carried on by leaders and organization. Bancroft had had no problem in stating the existence of leadership and organization in England; there was no democracy there. But he faced a philosophical problem in dealing with leadership and organization in colonies that theoretically were so perfectly democratic that the people ruled themselves. When Bancroft affirmed the existence of an aristocracy of wealth and talent which controlled the government of each colony and which began the political conflict with England in the 1760's, he was not embarrassing his theory of American history; he was protecting it. The people as innocents could not engage in political warfare. The conflict leading to 1776 must be carried on by men who were not pure or perfect.

Furthermore, Bancroft made the colonial aristocracy alien to the real people. During the centuries of British authority, this foreign influence had created an artificial class structure in the colonies. He cited the example of the decline of Virginia's primitive democracy: "If, in following years, she [Virginia] departed from either of these principles [religious and political equality] and yielded a reluctant consent to change, it was from the influence of foreign authority." [16]

There were then, in the 1760's, governing aristocracies in each colony which began to defend their selfish interests against the invasion of the equally selfish authority of the English governing aristocracy. Gradually, this conflict intensified until imperial England struck at the whole concept of free government with its imposition of the Intolerable Acts against Massachusetts. Suddenly this petty conflict over petty interests was transformed into a basic constitutional issue: Shall free government continue to exist in America? It became clear that free government could only be preserved by sundering all connections with monarchical and aristocratic England. And the colonial aristocracy shuddered at this prospect of independence in the name of democracy.

The people, however, faced with the ultimate crisis of losing democracy or declaring independence now took charge. Again Bancroft was sophisticated enough to describe a revolution with leadership and organization provided by the American aristocracy. But after 1776, the aristocracy were puppets in the hands of the people. "Of the American statesmen," he wrote, "who assisted to frame the new government, not one had been originally a republican. They had been as it were seized by the godlike spirit of freedom, and compelled to advance its banner." [17]

Among the American people, perfect and innocent, dynamic and creative leadership was impossible. Bancroft argued that if the people were free and equal in their opportunity to apprehend God's law, then they must respond freely and equally to whatever directions were given to them by God. They would move forward as a united body under the inspiration of

God. There were, however, representative men who were able to symbolize the virtues and values of the body politic and who acted as the agents of the will of the people.

Here in the crisis of revolution there emerged such a representative leader, George Washington. Bancroft made it clear that Washington was not a member of the colonial aristocracy. As the American people had stepped out of European history and had no past, so George Washington was an orphan. As the American people were without a cultural heritage and were shaped by nature, so was Washington: "At eleven years old, left an orphan to the care of an excellent but unlettered mother, he grew up without learning. . . . His culture was altogether his own work, and he was in the strictest sense a self-made man. . . . At sixteen he went into the wilderness as a surveyor, and for three years continued the pursuit, where the forests trained him, in meditative solitude, to freedom and largeness of mind; and nature revealed to him her obedience to serene and silent laws." [18] Again, as the people remained silent during the growing crisis between 1763 and 1775, so did Washington. When the people took control of the Revolution in that year, Washington, as one of the people, was ready to act with them. When the people asked him to represent them as their military leader, he was ready to accept that responsibility.

In Bancroft's chronicle of the Revolution, there emerged another representative leader almost as important as Washington, Daniel Boone. The symbolic importance of Daniel Boone rested upon the destiny of the American people to take over the area of the Mississippi Valley, the valley of democracy. It was God's intent that this vast area of nature be taken away from Old World authority and given to His children. As Washington was chosen to defeat the English in the East, Boone was chosen to lead the American occupation of the interior of the continent.

Completing this trinity of humble leaders of the humble God-fearing people was Thomas Jefferson. Jefferson, another simple country youth, was chosen to speak for the people when he wrote the Declaration of Independence: ". . . he was able with instinctive perception to read the soul of the nation, and having collected in himself its best thoughts and noblest feelings, to give them out in clear and bold words, mixed with so little of himself, that his country, as it went along with him, found nothing but what it recognized as its own. No man of his century had more trust in the collective reason and conscience of his fellow men." [19]

This was the final triumph of God's will in destroying the decadent forces of history. The American people had become the historical agents of His will and Washington, Boone, and Jefferson had become the agents of the people's will. American independence was the culmination of a cosmic spiritual revolution: "Virginia moved from charters and customs to primal principles; from a narrow altercation with lawyers about facts to the contemplation of immutable truth. She summoned the eternal laws of man's being to protest against all tyranny. The English petition of right in 1688, was historic and retrospective; the Virginia declaration came directly out of the heart of nature, and announced governing principles for all peoples in all future times. It was the voice of reason going forth to create new institutions, to speak a new political world into being." [20]

But Bancroft was caught in the rhythm of an ideology that could not fulfill itself. In the passage quoted above, he declared America the ideological capital of a world revolution to destroy the medieval past. But just as quickly, he withdrew the United States from this ideological responsibility. The Americans, as children of nature, were innocents who did not act in the world of historical conflict. Americans could not offer a revolutionary ideology to the rest of the nations because they had none. They had only the experience of stepping out of history into a state of nature. Here they had surrendered European theology and philosophy and political theory and had become the simple children of nature, obedient to the word of God and nature. America "in regenerating its institutions . . . was not guided by any speculative theory, or laborious application of metaphysical distinctions. . . . the formation of political institutions in the United States was not effected by giant minds . . . American history knows but one avenue to success in American legislation — freedom from ancient prejudice. The truly great law givers in our colonies first became as little children. . . . There can be no such thing as a creation of laws; for laws are but the arrangement of men in society in their just and natural relations. . . . with all the glad anticipations of greatness that broke forth from the prophetic soul of the youthful nation, they [the people] took their point of departure from the world as it was." [21]

If the Americans lived in a community where the ideal of God's law had become fact, then their chief responsibility was to defend and conserve this liberal way of life. They must recognize that they had not freely chosen this experience; it had been the gift of an omnipotent God. Their responsibility was to keep pure and undefiled this New World Garden of Eden, to keep any traces of European medievalism out of the Western hemisphere. Their responsibility was to keep this new covenant with God and God's nature. The American experience could stand as a beacon of inspiration to the rest of humanity which was still trapped by history. The rest of mankind could hope that God in His infinite wisdom and power would ultimately free them also from their medieval heritage to live in harmony with nature. But the other nations must wait patiently for God to act and Americans must wait patiently too, accepting their responsibility to preserve their innocence. We must accept this burden of liberal experience, this burden of innocence, Bancroft admonished his contemporaries, because "Here, and . . . here only, was a people . . . prepared to act as the depository and carrier of all political power. America developed her choice from within herself; and therefore it is, that, conscious of following an inner law, she never made herself a spreader of her own system." America was able to help Europe only by isolating herself from Europe.[22]

With something approaching desperation, Bancroft struggled to escape this logical trap which not only separated America but even God from Europe. Again and again he pointed out that Europe had "given to America her sons and culture. She was the mother of our men, and of the ideas which guided them to greatness." He repeatedly reaffirmed that Americans would repay this debt, sharing their revolution with their ancestors: "From the intelligence that had been slowly ripening in the mind of cultivated humanity, sprung the American Revolution, which was designed to organize social union through the establishment of personal freedom, and thus emancipate the nations from all authority not flowing from themselves."[23]

But as long as Bancroft explained the American escape from medieval history in terms of a frontier experience, his desire to see the American model copied in Europe must remain a pious hope. And he turned away from this insoluble problem that threatened to halt the march of God's progressive spirit in human history. He would concentrate on the progress of the United States itself.

Once more Bancroft seemed to be creating a logically contradictory philosophical problem. If the perfection of a natural society had been achieved in the first settlements and given national form in 1776, how then could America experience progress? Bancroft solved this problem with ease. The people had achieved democracy in the thirteen colonies along the east coast by living with nature. But Bancroft had demonstrated that a colonial aristocracy had developed in those colonies because of English influence. Historical complexity, a stratified social structure, had come to America from Europe.

During the Revolution itself, when the people had forced the aristocracy to lead them to independence, they had guaranteed the survival of the aristocracy. Because of the aristocracy's continued presence and leadership, the new state constitutions were imperfectly democratic. As the people went into the nineteenth century, they continued to be frustrated by the presence of men who were not the children of nature but who were still shaped by European culture. Inevitably, these undemocratic, unnatural men began to conspire to take away the people's liberties. Men of a privileged class, filled with English ideology, they decided to use institutional arrangements to imprison the people — that institutional structure centered around the Second Bank of the United States, an agency which represented English economic thought. Gradually these conspirators, through the first decades of the nineteenth century, spread their power over the economy, destroying the economic liberties of the people. The American principle of *laissez-faire* was being threatened by English capitalism.

Once more the American people, in the 1820's, must prepare to save their natural democracy from this threat of foreign tyranny even as their ancestors had done a half century before. But this was to be a popular revolution in defense of the Edenlike *status quo* which was to demonstrate that even where there was perfection, there was the possibility of progress. In 1775, against foreign tyranny, the people had been forced to use the leadership of the colonial aristocracy, with the exception of the chief American heroes, Washington, Boone, and Jefferson, who were children of the frontier. Now, however, because of the expanding frontier, the leadership of the Jacksonian revolution could be made up completely of the Washington kind of representative hero. By the 1820's, a number of western states had entered the union. Here in the valley of democracy, no colonial aristocracy existed. The English-dominated capitalists were all concentrated in the eastern cities. The political leaders of the western states were all common men, they had sprung from the people. The western states themselves, because they developed without the presence of the eastern aristocracy, were completely democratic in form.

From this absolutely pure Midwest would come representative leaders of the people who would rescue the people of the East from their temporary bondage to the artificial aristocracy which centered around the Bank of the United States. And the greatest of these representative leaders was, of course, Andrew Jackson. Like Washington, like the people, he was an "orphan hero" who in "infancy sported in the ancient forests, and his mind was nursed to freedom by their influence." Bancroft suggested that, in a way, Jackson had prepared for the epic struggle against the Second Bank by leaving the east coast of his childhood to help build the pure democracies of the Midwest. Here, led by Jackson, "The men of Tennessee, in less than twenty-five days, perfected a fabric, which, in its essential forms, was to last forever. They came together, full of faith and reverence, of love to humanity, of confidence in truth. In the simplicity of wisdom, they constructed their system, acting under higher influences than they were conscious of;

> They wrought in sad sincerity,
> Themselves from God they could not free;
> They builded better than they knew;
> The conscious stones to beauty grew." [24]

There was progress when men went west, when they turned their backs on the east coast which was partially contaminated by the European-influenced aristocracy. Here in Tennessee was created the first perfectly democratic state constitution. All of America, in contrast to Europe as history, was nature, but the trans-Appalachian West was more natural than the east coast.

Tennessee sent its representative hero, Jackson, to Congress and "This child of the woodlands, this representative of forest life in the West, appeared modestly and firmly on the side of liberty." Bancroft related that Jackson was immediately distressed by the evidence he saw that the eastern aristocracy was taking control of the national government. But, like the humble Washington, he would take no active role of leadership against this tyranny until the people called. Then he, too, accepted his responsibility to act as the people's agent. "Behold, then, the unlettered man of the West, the nursling of the wilds, the farmer of the Hermitage, little versed in books . . . raised by the will of the people to the highest pinnacle of honor, to the central post in the civilization of republican freedom, to the office where all the powers of the earth would watch his actions. . . . What policy will he pursue? What wisdom will he bring with him from the forest? . . . The man of the West came as the inspired prophet of the West; he came as one free from the bonds of hereditary or established custom. . . . he reverted from the pressure of established interests to the energy of first principles. . . . it was the office of Jackson to lift the country out of the European forms of legislation, and to open to it a career resting on American sentiment and American freedom." [25]

For Bancroft, it was a simple matter for Jackson to smash the Second Bank and to destroy the eastern aristocracy. After all, this was an institution and a class which were not truly American. This was an artificial and parasitical aristocracy which could be easily removed from the body politic of the people. Furthermore, Bancroft had to define the victory of Jackson in simple terms. An analysis of the institutional structure of the newly formed Democratic party, an analysis of Jackson as a party leader, an analysis of the role of professional politicians like Van Buren — all these would suggest that institutional complexity was to increase in America after 1828. The role of Jackson had to be that of the restorer of Jeffersonian simplicity. Jackson had restored the nation to its original purity; he had preserved the Jeffersonian covenant with nature; but he had brought revolutionary progress to the nation by moving its spiritual center from the polluted and complex East to the pure and primitive Mississippi Valley. For the first time, the national government was to be in the hands of the people, safe from any European influence. European tradition had infiltrated the East because of the centuries of British rule but it was never to cross the mountains into the valley of democracy. One would not dare defile this new Garden of Eden by describing it as the home of a political party.

As long as there was a frontier of primitive nature, Bancroft was able to promise that there would be spiritual progress. Given the vastness of the American West, there was even a way for the United States to share its blessing with Europeans, to let them leave history and come to nature. "Come, children of sorrow," Bancroft called, "you on whom the Old World frowns; crowd fearlessly to the forests, plant your homes in confidence." [26]

With the victory of Jackson, the people, and the West over the wicked aristocracy of the East, America was now totally delivered from the disharmony of history into the harmony of nature. With the obliteration of the influence of the last vestiges of European tradition and institutions, there could be no further problems in the United States. All was perfection.

Bancroft, however, like the average follower of Andrew Jackson, suppressed in his own mind the existence of an institution which violently contradicted the democratic affirmation of unqualified equality and freedom for all the people. Jacksonian America believed that social creativity was denied to Americans because they had achieved the perfect innocence of a state of nature. Jacksonian democracy, therefore, could not disestablish the massive institution of slavery. Such an undertaking would necessitate social and economic planning; it required political action by government and that would violate *laissez-faire*. Bancroft and his democratic contemporaries of the 1830's had to be content with democracy for white men only. He had not ignored slavery in his historical writing. He found it a terrible burden imposed upon the innocent and democratic Americans by the tyrannical British monarchy. But as a practical Jacksonian politician, he refused to talk about its moral implications for the present generation.

Like his fellow Americans, Bancroft lived with a troubled conscience until suddenly he and they found themselves engaged in a civil war that might end the evil of slavery. War was to become the agency of social revolution to achieve perfect democracy in America where, with slavery abolished, there would be no institutions or restraints upon any individual, white or black.

Again, Bancroft's historical description preserved the American burden of innocence. The people did not choose to act, even to end the moral evil of slavery. In the South, Bancroft wrote, there existed an un-American slaveholding aristocracy. Inevitably, it began to wage war on democracy by attempting to force the people to accept the legality of slavery everywhere in the country. When this slavocracy became aware that its aggressive antidemocratic ambitions had been defeated in the election of 1860, it decided, in its frustration and hatred, to destroy the nation and destroy God's great experiment in democracy.

How would the people react to this challenge to their democracy by this European-inspired aristocracy? The professional politicians had failed to meet and solve the crisis. The crowned heads of Europe sat like expectant vultures waiting to feast on the soon-to-be destroyed democracy. But the people, without professional leadership in this moment of crisis, were not afraid. They put their trust in God and acted according to His will. Once more they found a representative hero in their own bosom, an orphan of the frontier like Washington and Jackson, "one whose wisdom was like the wisdom of little children . . . the choice of America fell on a man born west of the Alleghanies, in the cabin of poor people of Harden county, Kentucky — Abraham Lincoln." The people chose Lincoln as their representative hero because he had "lived the life of the American people, walked in its light, reasoned with its reason, thought with its power of thought, felt the beating of its mighty heart, and so was in every way a child of nature, a child of the West, a child of America." [27]

Lincoln pledged himself to preserve the Union which represented God's republican goal for all humanity. He realized that the United States symbolized this ideal for all the peoples of the earth and that the progress of mankind toward this goal might suffer a mortal setback if the nation were destroyed. Lincoln then set himself on the course of preserving the Union against the rebellion of the slavocracy and looked to the people and to God for the strength to win. He did not look in vain: "When it came home to the consciousness of the Americans that the war which they were waging was a war for the liberty of all the nations of the world, for freedom itself, they thanked God for giving them strength to endure the severity of the trial to which He put their sincerity, and nerved themselves for their duty with an inexorable will. The President was led along by the greatness of their self-sacrificing example; and as a child, in a dark night, on a rugged way, catches hold of the hand of its father for guidance and support, he clung fast to the hand of the people, and moved calmly through the gloom." [28]

It was preordained, for Bancroft, that the American people, representing God, should defeat the slavocracy and free the slaves. Bancroft, who had ended American history in 1776 and 1828, proclaimed that finally the American millennium had arrived in 1865. Abraham Lincoln had destroyed the un-American slavocracy and the foreign institution of slavery. He had restored to original purity the principles of the Declaration of Independence. He had successfully defended the Jeffersonian covenant. And Bancroft promised that there could be no further threat to the covenant: ". . . for now slavery is no more, the Union is restored, a people begins to live according to the laws of reason, and republicanism is intrenched in a continent." [29]

3 FREDERICK JACKSON TURNER: THE MACHINE AND THE LOSS OF THE COVENANT

In 1865, George Bancroft promised Americans that they had witnessed their last historical crisis. He promised that now they would dwell in timeless simplicity and harmony forever. But before he died in 1891, Americans had experienced the greatest social and economic transformation in the history of mankind. An essentially rural society had suddenly become a fantastically complex urban-industrial community. Bancroft had promised that a democratic society of free and equal individuals, a classless society, would endure forever. By 1891, however, there were signs that the United States had a new class of the very rich and, equally disturbing, a class of the very poor.

The people of the 1890's needed a new political philosopher, a new historian to explain what had gone wrong since 1865. He turned out to be a young historian from the University of Wisconsin, Frederick Jackson Turner.

The new urban-industrial society, which should not have appeared in a changeless America, had raised gigantic cities on the midwestern prairies. It had also caused tremendous specialization and professionalization in the nation's academic establishment. In 1893, these revolutionary currents were blended as the newly formed American Historical Association met in Chicago, changed from a village to a metropolis of a million in a single generation. Here Turner presented his paper on "The Significance of the Frontier in America," a document that provided scientific sanction for Bancroft's theory of American history, explained the cultural dilemma of the country in the 1890's, and captured the imagination of the reading public as well as the historical profession.

37

The superintendent of the census of 1890, said Turner in his paper, has reported that there is no longer a frontier line in America. "This brief official statement marks the closing of a great historic movement. Up to our own day American history has been in a large degree the history of the colonization of the Great West. The existence of an area of free land, its continuous recession, and the advance of American settlement westward, explain American development." [1] Here was the explanation of why Bancroft had failed to prophesy the gigantic changes after the Civil War. The frontier was gone; it was as simple as that. The Jeffersonian promise of a frontier that would last into the indefinite future had failed of fulfillment. America had lost contact with that nature which had guaranteed the absence of complexity of the European type.

Turner tried to suggest that Americans should find satisfaction in the loss of their national covenant with nature. Bancroft had postulated that the law of history was progress. By the 1870's, men had learned that there was a scientific law of evolution. Human evolution was movement from simplicity to complexity, from the primitive to the civilized. If America had moved from the agrarian frontier to an urban-industrial frontier, from youth to maturity, this was the law of evolution and this must be progress. As a scholar interested in discovering laws of human behavior, irrespective of national boundaries, Turner seemed to rejoice in the dramatic picture of social evolution that was nineteenth-century America. After all, he argued, the Italian economist Loria has pointed out that all societies go through a series of fixed stages as they move from their childhood to an adult state. By looking at the transformation of the American frontier, one can understand the evolution of human society everywhere: "Loria . . . has urged the study of colonial life as an aid to understanding the stages of European development. . . . There is much truth in this. The United States lies like a huge page in the history of society. Line by line as we read this continental page from West to East we find the record of social evolution." [2] But this affirmation of intellectual satisfaction with evolution and progress did not disguise the frightening implication of Turner's essay that the achievement of civilization was offset by the loss of democracy.

If, as Turner believed, "American democracy was born of no theorist's dream . . . It came stark and strong and full of life out of the American forest and it gained new strength each time it touched a new frontier," [3] then the triumphant spread of civilization from Europe across the face of the United States, this triumph of progress over primitivism, inexorably doomed the national democratic covenant with nature. For Turner as for Bancroft, the transformation of the European into the American democrat had been a religious experience of rebirth which depended upon the mystical powers of virgin land: "Into this vast shaggy continent of ours poured the first feeble tide of European settlement. European men, institutions, and ideas were lodged in the American wilderness, and this great American West took them to her bosom, taught them a new way of looking upon the destiny of the common man, trained them in adaptation to the conditions of the New World, to the creation of new institutions to meet new needs; and ever as society on her eastern border grew to resemble the Old World in its social forms and its industry, ever, as it began to lose faith in the ideal of democracy, she opened new provinces, and dowered new democracies in her most distant domains with her material treasures and with the enobling influence that the fierce love of freedom . . . furnished to the pioneer." [4]

Like Bancroft, Turner endowed physical nature in America with the fruitfulness of the feminine gender; nature was feminine. Like Bancroft, he described Europe as neuter. American democracy was, therefore, losing its fruitfulness as it lost nature. It was becoming sterile as it came to imitate Europe. Bancroft believed in a progress that reached constantly toward the primitivism of the West. As Turner had reached maturity, however, the primitive West disappeared. He would try to persuade himself and his generation that change toward the complexity of the East was progress, that the ideal of civilization was more valid than the ideal of primitivism. He would fail.

Frederick Jackson Turner was born in Portage, Wisconsin, in 1861. Fascinated by history, he had studied the ancient past at the University of Wisconsin with Professor William F. Allen, a specialist in Roman history, who, in turn, had studied with Bancroft's teacher, Heeren, at Göttingen. From Wisconsin, Turner journeyed east to Johns Hopkins to study with the German-trained Herbert Baxter Adams, who had established the first German-type seminar of historical study in America. Adams was demonstrating through the newest critical and scientific methods that American democratic institutions were expressions of ancient German practices, originated by the primitive Anglo-Saxons in the Teutonic forests. Turner went to learn truths that he already believed. He fully shared Bancroft's theory that among the Europeans it was only the Anglo-Saxons who could achieve harmony with nature in the New World because they had not allowed the corrupt institutions of medieval civilization to destroy their roots in the purity and simplicity of the primitive state of nature which was the primeval forest environment of northwestern Europe. Henry Nash Smith has pointed out that Turner wrote in a book review in 1889 that "the old Germanic 'tun' " reappeared in the "forted village" of early Kentucky and Tennessee, the "folkmoot" in popular meetings of the settlers and the "witenagemot" in representative assemblies like the Transylvania legislature. "These facts carry the mind back to the warrior-legislatures in the Germanic forests, and forward to those constitutional conventions now at work in our own newly-made states in the Far West; and they make us proud of our English heritage." [5]

Though Turner might later write, in the same vein, that "Our early history is the study of European germs developing in an American environment," his emphasis, like Bancroft's, would be on the American environment and he would also write, "Too exclusive attention has been paid by institutional students to Germanic origins, too little to the American factors." [6]

When Turner began to prove Bancroft's conclusions, he failed to include in his historical writings many of the theological and philosophical assumptions that were such a fundamental part of Bancroft's historical approach. But from the moment Turner wrote in his youthful commonplace book that history had culminated in the triumph of the common man, it was clear that his historical interpretation was an act of faith which rested on much the same metaphysical and theological foundation that supported Bancroft's view of history. His first major essay after receiving his doctorate was called "The Significance of History." Published in 1891, it provides the intellectual context for his epic-making address of 1893 and demonstrates the way in which his apparent geographic or economic interpretation of history rests on the foundation of philosophical idealism.

In the past, he wrote, history has been conceived as literary art or the chronicle of past politics. Today, however, we are coming to define history as fundamentally the story of economic development. We have learned, he continued, to understand the importance of man's economic life because of the influence of the German philosophers of the early nineteenth century. Turner now asked his colleagues to accept the authority of the philosophical idealists to whom Bancroft had paid homage. These German scholars have demonstrated, wrote Turner, that the evolution of society proceeds according to laws beyond human control; they have demonstrated "that the state is not in reality governed by laws of man's devising, but is part of the moral order of the universe, ruled by cosmic forces from above." Turner had rediscovered Bancroft's doctrine of predestination. The scientific historian, Turner continued, discovered and made clear the laws of social evolution. The concept of scientific history, he stated, originated with Herder and found its first practical expression in the writings of Niebuhr who believed "in the growth of an institution according to fixed laws." Today, he concluded, most historians have accepted "the doctrine of Herder. Society grows. They have accepted the doctrine of Comte. Society is an organism." [7]

Turner was an economic determinist because he saw history as determined by God. And, like Bancroft, he saw the basic economic factor in America to be free land, virgin land, nature. Turner was a geographic determinist because he was a philosophical idealist. Like Bancroft, he believed that the spiritual force of the universe had found fulfillment within the context of America's geography.

And this was Turner's dilemma as it was that of the nation. Industrialism had replaced the physical frontier as the central economic force by 1890. According to Turner, this new economic order must express the will of God; it was beyond human control. Turner could find no way to interpret the change which had occurred between 1865 and 1890 as one of Bancroft's moral dramas. He was not able to argue that an alien group was conspiring to destroy American democracy and introduce European complexity. He could not write a Jeremiad to rally the people to a puritanical defense of the national covenant. Industrialism was natural; it was not artificial as Bancroft's enemy, the Second Bank of the United States, had been. Desperately, Turner reworked Bancroft's historical interpretation. He was consciously to examine the possibility that the new complexity was artificial and alien and could be swept away; he was to reject that hope. He was consciously to examine the possibility that since the new complexity was impersonal and real and not institutional and artificial, it did not threaten our national covenant with nature. This hope he also rejected. Turner's historical writing was never to become more than a nostalgic and loving backward glance at the creation of the American Garden in 1830 and a sorrowful commentary on a disharmonious present.

Turner began his historical writing in agreement with Bancroft that Englishmen had stepped out of history and into a state of nature in 1607. There was an American people, an American democracy, produced by the first frontier. This people was made up of free and equal individuals, liberated from European traditions and institutions. He agreed with Bancroft that the only real change that could occur in the lives of these redeemed men would be that caused by European influence. But he stressed much more than Bancroft had the existence of a colonial aristocracy that grew out of English interference. He associated this colonial aristocracy, including Washington, much more closely with the events of the Revolution and the writing of the imperfectly democratic state and national constitutions. For Bancroft, most of the primitive democracy of 1600 had been restored by 1776. For Turner, the epic struggle to restore the Garden of Eden was that waged by the people against the colonial aristocracy between 1776 and 1828. For Bancroft, George Washington was the chief hero of the people. For Turner, it was Andrew Jackson. The central drama of American history for Bancroft was the struggle of the people against European influence as represented by British officialdom, and this ended in 1776. The central drama of American history for Turner was the struggle of the people against European influence as represented by the colonial aristocracy, and this ended in 1828. Most of Bancroft's history was written about the period before 1776; most of Turner's history was written about the period 1800–1830.

Turner described the early appearance of the "people" in the seventeenth century in an essay called "The First Official Frontier of the Massachusetts Bay." In Massachusetts and Virginia, he wrote, there were, by the 1640's, individuals living at the edge of the civilized communities who were soon to be precipitated into a state of primitivism and then, he added, began "The common sequence of frontier types . . . the cattle-raising pioneer, the small primitive farmer, and the farmer engaged in intensive varied agriculture to produce a surplus for export." [8] Here, he declared, appeared the first American expressions of individualism and democracy, the first typical frontier hostility to the established order of the East. Here, on the frontier, one found in Bacon's rebellion the first attempt of the people to overthrow both British authority and the colonial aristocracy.

Gradually, however, eastern authority pushed inland to the fall line of the rivers and ended the existence of this first frontier. But, immediately, there appeared a larger and more vigorously democratic frontier, one Turner called "the Old West," which extended west from the fall line of the rivers to the crest of the Appalachians and which reached from backcountry New England to Georgia. Now truly, "A new society had been established, differing in essentials from the colonial society of the coast. It was a democratic, self-sufficing, primitive agricultural society." [9] He found that this new society was in constant conflict with "the party of privilege, chiefly the Eastern men of property allied with the English authorities." He also found that the intensity of this conflict between the democratic West and the aristocratic East was growing throughout the eighteenth century; it exploded in physical violence in the War of the Regulators against the North Carolina aristocracy.

Turner was explicitly defining the process of westward expansion as progress; he argued that each succeeding frontier experience made the people more democratic and more American. And he agreed with Bancroft that complete and uncorrupted Americanism was achieved first in the Midwest. Turner made it clear that "the settlements from the mountains to the seaboard kept connection with the rear." It was only "from the time the mountains rose between the pioneer and the seaboard" that "a new order of Americanism arose." [10] European civilization did not cease to color the American experience until the primitivism of the Mississippi Valley took absolute control of the pioneer.

By bringing American history to a climax in the 1820's with the development of a trans-Appalachian society of a purified people, Turner avoided the awkward arguments by which Bancroft had to demonstrate that, while American history had reached total fulfillment in 1776, it was necessary to repeat that fulfillment in 1828. Turner did not declare that pure democracy had been established during the Revolution. Instead he argued that there were two struggles taking place during the years 1775–1783: the struggle of the people to overthrow English authority and their struggle to overthrow the colonial aristocracy. This latter struggle he defined in largely sectional terms. It was the democracy of the "Old West" against the aristocracy of the east coast. The aristocracy survived this battle for the control of the new nation and wrote the Constitution and took direction of the federal government in the 1790's. For Turner, the European-influenced eastern aristocracy dominated national history until 1800.

In 1800, Thomas Jefferson became president of the United States and struck the first major blow against this un-American upper class. As Bancroft had removed Washington from the ranks of the eastern aristocracy to make him a spokesman of the people, so Turner now lifted Jefferson out of his aristocratic context to describe him as a simple frontier farmer.

"Jefferson," Turner wrote, "was the first prophet of American democracy, and when we analyze the essential features of his gospel, it is clear that the Western influence was the dominant element." [11] By the logic of his argument, Jefferson's presidency must have been accidental because Turner found no revolutionary overthrow of the eastern class structure in 1800. Instead he argued that Jefferson was not able to lead the country to democracy because the trans-Appalachian frontier had not as yet produced enough natural democrats to outvote the eastern aristocracy at the polls. Jefferson, he declared, was but "the John the Baptist of democracy, not its Moses. Only with the slow settling of the tide of settlement farther and farther toward the interior did the democratic influence grow strong enough to take actual possession of the government." [12] In 1828, not 1776, came the culmination of American history. But this history of progress was not the history of change, of novelty, of confusion, or complexity because it was the history of the fulfillment of that natural potential which had existed in the virgin land of the continent from the very beginning of settlement, the fulfillment of the natural democracy of a people which had escaped from European history.

It is fascinating to watch Turner, the careful and objective historian, arrange the complex and conflicting facts of the American historical experience so that, ultimately, they would fit neatly into the patterns of Bancroft's faith. As a historian, Turner had to describe the dynamic changes of the American scene. As the theologian and political philosopher of democracy, he must demonstrate that this record of change did not violate the changelessness of the American covenant with nature.

Turner's two books of narrative history inevitably dealt with the first half of the nineteenth century. They are *The Rise of the New West, 1819–1828* and *The United States, 1830–1850.*

He began the first book with the affirmation that the years 1819–1829 were the most important in our history because they marked the final achievement of total independence from the Old World. It was then that democracy, the rule of the people, triumphed and America fulfilled her destiny. The force responsible for this revolution was the rise to power of the western states. Here the "people" ruled and they now turned back to the East to provide leadership for the fellow common men along the seaboard. They helped the suppressed "people" of the old states to overthrow aristocratic rule. Andrew Jackson represented not just the West, but the only American social class, the "people."

With illuminating candor, Turner confessed that he could not describe the process by which the western people had overthrown the rule of the eastern aristocracy. Was it because such a description would necessarily involve analysis of the political institutions of the period? Would Turner have been forced to deal with the hypothesis that it was the emergence of national political parties and professional politicians which provided the institutional structure and leadership necessary to mobilize the people as a formal majority that could vote the aristocracy out of office? The essence of the Jeffersonian covenant was that the institutional structure of the Old World had withered away in the New World and that no new institutional structure was to appear. Could the historian of Jacksonian democracy then admit that democracy had appeared because of the appearance of new institutions? Could the historian of Jacksonian democracy admit that the free and equal people were being led by a new, specialized group of professional politicians? It is significant that Bancroft had also described the triumph of Jacksonian democracy as a spontaneous uprising of the people, almost completely ignoring the positive role of the political party and the professional politician.

Turner did not try to explain his statement that he was not able to describe the mechanics of the democratic triumph. Instead he turned to those aspects of the decade he was able to describe without threatening the Jeffersonian covenant. In a book that announced the importance of the new West, Turner described the changes that were taking place in New England and the old South. Here were two regions that had developed for two hundred years under European influence and where change might be defined as progress.

The most significant changes in New England, he wrote, were economic. Agriculture was declining drastically under competition from the new West and commercial leaders were investing their surplus capital in manufacturing. By the end of the 1820's, New England was dominated by the new economic force of industrialism and her representatives had taken a strong stand for a high tariff and national banking. The old South, he continued, had become committed during this same period to the production of cotton. By the end of the 1820's, the South had, therefore, turned against the tariff and national banking.

Turner had created a picture of the nation in 1828 dominated by two monolithic sections in absolute economic competition with one another. If Turner was not able to describe the institutional process by which the

Democratic party brought political democracy to the country in 1828, he could describe the noninstitutional way in which the divided nation might be preserved by the common man of the West. The New Englander was concerned only with the interests of his region. The southerner was concerned only with the interests of his region. Because of the selfish outlook of these older regions, the nation seemed about to fall apart. But western pioneers transcended their regional interest to affirm the unity of the entire nation as the proper seat of a great democratic experiment. It was the will of these men, as represented in Andrew Jackson, which preserved the unity of the nation. The common men "of the growing west were rallying around the man who personified their passion for democracy and nationalism — the fiery Jackson. . . . This frontiersman was little likely to allow political metaphysics . . . to check his will." [13] Calhoun's political theory of nullification had to bow to Jackson's will, and the nation, as an experiment in democracy, was to be preserved as long as Jackson was president. Ultimately, of course, this Old Hero must pass from the scene and then the divisive forces of New England and the South were to break loose again. But Turner had a word of final reassurance for his reader; remember, he implored, the infinite regenerative power of the West, old heroes of the West must be replaced by new. "And on the frontier of the northwest, the young Lincoln sank his axe deep in the opposing forest." [14]

The final sentiment of the first book provides the key for understanding the philosophical changes Turner made in the sequel, *The United States, 1830–1850.* At the end of *The Rise of the New West,* he was faced with major philosophical and historical problems. There was a conflict in Turner's mind because of his commitment to both savagery and civilization. He believed that democracy came about when a complex society was simplified by contact with a primitive or savage state of nature, with an unsettled frontier. He also believed that human history was the inevitable upward movement from primitive conditions to civilization. Turner was faced then with the philosophical dilemma that the progress toward civilization in which he believed as both inevitable and good seemed necessarily to destroy the natural basis for that democracy to which he so passionately adhered. In *The Rise of the New West,* he had found democracy triumphant on the frontier west of the mountains — but, by the end of the book, he was describing the advance of complex economic and social patterns from the East into the Mississippi Valley. The strength of the valley of democracy was threatened just at the moment when its historical mission was most urgent. Surely it was the destiny of democracy to triumph in the world, surely then it must conquer all of the United States. It must obliterate the traditional attitudes and institutional arrangement of New England and the South in order to create a totally democratic nation. Somehow, for Turner, as institutional complexity flowed from the east to the west, democracy must flow from the west to the east and must triumph.

Turner began to solve these problems in the second book by defining the regions in a different fashion. In *The Rise of the New West,* New England had been the chief enemy of the democratic West because it was the stronghold of the colonial aristocracy. But now, in this later book, Turner found the major threat to democracy located in the South. Because of the South, there was no longer a western region stretching the length of the Mississippi Valley. The alien institution, slavery, which provided the basis for an alien class, the planter aristocracy, had invaded the Mississippi Valley and destroyed the democratic communities of the southern frontier. In the new Southwest as in the old Southeast, the common men, "the people," were submerged by a planter class. Democracy could not triumph in the South from Virginia to Texas until slavery was abolished and the planter aristocracy destroyed.

But while the institutions of the Old South were moving across the mountains to corrupt the southern part of the valley of democracy, Federalist New England was losing its aristocracy; it was being freed from its historical past and was being redeemed by its contact with that part of the West which remained pure, the Midwest. It was with pleased surprise that Turner reported that when the commercial aristocracy of New England had created industrialism in its region, it had committed social, political, and intellectual suicide because industry "broke the crust of custom" and allowed her people to share "more fully in the temper of the nation." [15]

Turner then turned to enlarging his definition of democracy. He had begun this book defining democracy in purely agricultural terms. He had written of the Jacksonian triumph that "It meant that an agricultural society, strongest in the areas of rural isolation rather than in the areas of greater density of population and of greater wealth, had triumphed, for the time, over the conservative, industrial, commercial, and manufacturing society of the New England type. It meant that a new aggressive, expansive democracy, emphasizing human rights and individualism, as against the old established order which emphasized vested rights and corporate action, had come into control." [16] As the book progressed, however, it became clear that he was changing his definition of democracy to include complex economic and social activity which had a relation to New England. Turner now found that the Midwest, the citadel of American democracy, was tied historically to New England. Analyzing the background of the people of the Midwest, Turner declared they had come from two major sources: first from New England and then, later, from Germany.

The New Englanders who had come west were "the common people" of their region, committed to democracy and antagonistic to the established aristocracy they left behind. Like the common men from the South who had come west, they "made a creed of innovation," they were "impatient with technicality," they preferred "vigor of action," and they distrusted "government by a trained and established class." But unlike the anarchistic pioneers from the South, the New Englanders understood that cooperation must be the essence of any healthy community. They understood that equality demanded a limitation of individualism.

This New England definition of frontier democracy as community cooperation was reinforced by the German pioneers. They too had fled from aristocratic overlords to find freedom in the wilderness; they too defined freedom in cooperative terms. The "cross-fertilization" of New Englander and German was creating a self-conscious community in the Midwest which "believed it was to shape the nation's ideals and society into a New World in all ways," [17] not only politically but also economically. Turner had decided that an industrialism and urbanism which sprang from a free people must be good and he applauded the pioneer of the Northwest in these terms: "Side by side with this westward marching army of individualistic liberty-loving democratic backwoods men, went a more Northern stream of pioneers, who cherished similar ideas, but added to them the desire to create new industrial centers, to build up factories . . . to develop the country by founding cities and extending prosperity." [18]

Evidently, Turner was developing a historical formula that might reconcile progress and primitivism. Complexity might not threaten primitive democracy if it was the direct product of "the people" themselves. If complexity in the Midwest was not the result of outside forces from the East, but was indigenous to its perfected democracy, then it might be safe. And since industrialism had broken the established control of aristocracy in New England and had liberated its people, the people were able to gain democratic inspiration from their cousins who had created midwestern

culture. New England was redeemed and became in the 1830's and 1840's
the literary center of the new democracy. New England literature now
reflected "the spirit of Jacksonian Democracy, with its exaltation of the
individual and its break with the past. . . . Beyond any other New Englander, Emerson caught the spirit of the New West . . . the belief in the
perfectibility of the common man, the connection of wagon and star, the
appeal to the imagination made by vast spaces, affording opportunity for
a newer and finer society." [19]

Turner never completed the manuscript of this book but he set the direction of the American chronicle so that his readers were able to understand the drama of the years that immediately followed 1850, culminating
in the Civil War. He had lifted Abraham Lincoln out of the stream of immigration that had come from the South into the Midwest and related him
to the Midwest of New England and German democracy. Lincoln, wrote
Turner, did not share the philosophy of extreme individualism held by the
southern pioneer. Rather, from his childhood, he had stood apart from
his fellow pioneers, instinctively believing in the community-centered democracy of the New England part of the Midwest. He also shared the New
England viewpoint of economic growth and progress. It was Lincoln who
expressed the sense of midwestern democracy when he told the South that
the nation could not exist half slave and half free. And it was the destiny
of this "free pioneer democracy," led by Lincoln, to strike "down the
slave-holding aristocracy on its march to the West."

With the coming of the Civil War, Lincoln and the Midwest took over
the national government, emancipated the slaves, and destroyed the southern aristocracy. The Civil War, then, marked the national triumph of midwestern democracy. It had liberated New England before the war; it now
liberated the South. Turner's historical imagination blended with that of
Bancroft as he visualized this final and complete triumph of natural democracy. Now, in 1865, Americans had achieved final harmony with nature. The institutions and traditions of the eastern aristocracy were obliterated. There was to be no further record of development in a land of
completely free and equal individuals. But Turner, unlike Bancroft, was
writing during the years 1890–1920, years when one could not ignore the
fantastic transformation of the United States into the world's mightiest industrial nation. He had to take into account the massive developments
and changes after 1865. Something was happening in America. Would

these transformations destroy the stability of the established democracy of 1865?

Indeed, this was the crucial question for Turner as an eyewitness to the history of his own times. As his two books of narrative history were concerned with the emergence of democracy in the early nineteenth century, so his essays in the popular journals at the beginning of the twentieth century were concerned with the threat that industrialism held for that democracy. Turner was obviously not satisfied with his own optimistic assertion that industrial complexity, growing directly from midwestern democracy, could not harm its parent source. He had to confess that the industrial revolution had begun in Europe, had spread to the east coast, and was now infiltrating the Midwest. Again and again, he asked himself and his contemporaries this haunting question: "Under the forms of the American democracy is there in reality evolving such a concentration of economic and social power in the hands of a comparatively few men as may make political democracy an appearance rather than a reality?" For Turner, this question was laden with still more frightening implications because if a new eastern aristocracy was appearing, there was now no area of virgin land to reinvigorate democracy. Tragically, Turner declared, "The free lands are gone. The material forces that gave vitality to Western democracy are passing away." [20]

How then was American democracy to be preserved? Turner's attempt at an answer reveals once more the relationship between his apparent geographic and economic determinism and his commitment to a position of philosophical idealism that again brought him very close to George Bancroft. "It is to the realm of the spirit, to the domain of ideals and legislation," he wrote, "that we must look for Western influence upon democracy in our own days." [21]

He now made it very clear that American democracy was the product of an idealism that had existed in Europe at the beginning of the seventeenth century. It was an idealism that was most clearly identified among the English Puritans. And here at the end of the nineteenth century, it was most visible among the Populists, who had been able to preserve their inherited Calvinist idealism because they had lived most closely with nature. Turner found a thread of connection between England's Cromwell and Mary Lease of Kansas in the flow of Puritan culture westward. "The Populist," he wrote, "is the American farmer who has kept in advance of the economic and social transformations that have overtaken those who remained behind." And he added, "If New England looks with care at these men, she may recognize in them the familiar lineaments of the embattled farmers who fired the shot heard round the world. The continuous advance of this pioneer stock from New England has preserved for us the older type of the pioneer of frontier New England. . . . In the arid West these pioneers have halted and have turned to perceive an altered nation and changed social ideals. They see the sharp contrast between their traditional idea of America, as the land of opportunity, the land of the self-made man, free from class distinctions and from the power of wealth, and the existing America, so unlike the earlier ideal. If we follow back the line of march of the Puritan farmer, we shall see how responsive he has always been to isms, and how persistently he has resisted encroachments on his ideals of individual opportunity and democracy. . . . If the voice of Mary Ellen Lease sounds raucous to the New England man today, while it is sweet music in the ears of the Kansas farmer, let him ponder the utterances of these frontier farmers in the days of the Revolution; and if he is still doubtful of this spiritual kinship, let him read the words of the levelers and sectaries of Cromwell's army." [22]

For Turner, then, the American Populist was our greatest liberal and, at the same time, our greatest conservative. The Populist problem "is not to create democracy, but to conserve democratic institutions and ideals." The Populist, Turner declared, had recognized by 1890 that the preservation of these ideals demanded a new attitude toward government. He must use the government to control the economy and society so that the old way of life was not smashed by the forces of industrialism and wealth.

Turner rejected the foreign ideology of socialism in this battle to save the western democracy of free and equal individuals from the threat of an eastern aristocracy. Socialism, he wrote, surrenders the freedom of the individual to coercive institutional regimentation. But as he carefully distinguished American democracy, the child of nature, from the European philosophy born of history, he also clearly identified the eastern aristocracy with a foreign ideology, capitalism, that had no place in an America that should be free from all European traditions. The European tradition of capitalism he defined as a philosophy of economic self-interest which destroyed the community by glorifying the law of unrestrained competition. Turner wanted a middle way, a "governmental discipline . . . which proceeds from free choice, in the conviction that restraint of individual or class interests is necessary for the common good." He found that this commonsense attitude toward social control existed in America before the Civil War among the pioneers who believed that "the distinction arising from devotion to the interests of the commonwealth is a higher distinction than mere success in economic competition." [23]

Turner might hope that capitalistic aristocracy, as an artificial entity without fundamental strength, could be as easily smashed and brushed away as Jackson had destroyed the eastern financial aristocracy during the 1830's without disturbing the essential structure of the nation. But he had to admit that the reappearance of a capitalist aristocracy in the East threatened the existence of American democracy in a way that was not to be as easily resolved as the crisis of the 1830's. Then the aristocracy had but one institution, the Second Bank of the United States, with which to attack the people. Andrew Jackson had a dragon with but a single head to destroy. Now the financial aristocracy was interrelated with industrialism. And industrialism had an infinite number of bodies and heads. Could one destroy the financial aristocracy without destroying the economic structure of the nation? The horrifying truth that Turner was no longer able to avoid was that industrialism was an impersonal economic force that was inexorably proving stronger than the economic force of the frontier.

Turner, like Bancroft, had enthusiastically accepted the doctrine of the German philosophers "that the state is not in reality governed by laws of man's devising" as long as this meant that the frontier as nature was destroying the artificialities of European culture. Turner had enthusiastically called for the study of the impersonal forces of economic history as long as the major economic force in American experience was free land. Now Turner was trapped by his own philosophy of predestination as well as by his philosophy of the anti-institutional character of American democracy.

Timidly, he had suggested a new political approach, that of Populism: to use legislation to control the impersonal forces of industrialism in the interests of a democratic society. But such an approach violated his belief that legislation cannot control the shape of society. Furthermore, to build a set of powerful political institutions to control the economy, even if this were done in the spirit of cooperative democracy rather than socialism, would violate the definition of American democracy as the absence of institutional structure. Turner was in the impossible position of arguing that Americans should artificially control their social environment when all his historical theory was opposed to such artificial control.

Not surprisingly, Turner began quietly to abandon his qualified endorsement of political power. Like Bancroft's, his view of the American as an innocent made it almost impossible for him to think of asking the American to accept the responsibility of power, especially institutionalized power with its inevitable corollary of professional leadership. Turner, like Bancroft, was able to accept the exercise of power in a spontaneous uprising of the people led by a representative hero. But how could a popular uprising disestablish industrialism? Whenever the people had rebelled in Bancroft's and Turner's histories, they had acted as the agents of nature to destroy an artificial and parasitic sore on the body politic. They had preserved the material *status quo* of nature. Now, however, the material *status quo* was industrialism. And Turner did not believe that political revolution was able to control economic forces. In 1890, there could be no natural revolution to conserve the *status quo* by destroying the irrelevant and insubstantial factor of European capitalistic ideology. That ideology was now materialized in industrialism; it had become the relevant and substantial reality of America.

Turner had to retreat to another line of defense. If political action was contrary to the spontaneity of American democracy, perhaps the area of education was not. In the Midwest, Turner wrote, there had appeared a unique educational institution, the state university. Unlike the political party, it was completely responsive to the people; it represented and served the entire community. Perhaps, he argued, this organ of the people might re-create a frontier of economic opportunity through applied scientific research. The safety valve of free land might be replaced with that of the laboratory. This was the last hope of checking the development of a hierarchical class structure in which both the plutocracy and the proletariat were without commitment to American democratic ideals. Hopefully, Turner asked that the midwestern state university produce national leaders who would keep the plutocracy from controlling the nation; he asked too that the university provide the educational and economic opportunities that would lift men out of the proletariat and teach them the values of a classless middle-class America. From these universities must come leaders, representative of the people, who could "preserve and entrench" democratic ideals "by courageous adaptations to new conditions" and provide "bulwarks against both the passionate impulses of the mob and the sinister designs of those who would subordinate public welfare to private greed." [24]

Like Bancroft, Turner continued to believe that the United States should serve as a beacon for all mankind to advance toward. Still clinging to a hope that history was progress, he interpreted World War I as the possible liberation of the European people from medieval darkness into a world made safe for democracy by American participation in a League for Nations dedicated to peace. But, like Bancroft in 1830, Turner could provide no logical argument for European progress when progress depended upon the presence of a physical frontier. Indeed in 1918, what hope for progress remained anywhere when even the American frontier had disappeared?

The midwestern frontier between 1789 and 1865, he repeated, presented mankind with a momentary chance to escape from history. Before 1789, men in America and Europe were ruled by complex traditions and institutions inherited from the past. After 1865, a new complexity began to develop in the wake of the industrial revolution. Turner found, therefore, that "Never again can such an opportunity come to the sons of men. It was unique." Since the ideal of democracy had found a proper material context only in the American Midwest, it was only here that the ideal had a chance to be defended. "It is in the vast and level spaces of the Mississippi Valley, if anywhere," Turner asserted, "that the forces of social transformation and the modification of its democratic ideals may be arrested." [25]

Turner, following the tradition of Bancroft, affirmed that democratic revolution is possible only by stepping out of history, not by destroying history by force. Europe, for Turner, had tried "to create an artificial democratic order by legislation," and it, of course, had to fail. Democracy must be found, not created. "We have believed," Turner continued, "that other peoples had only to will our democratic institutions in order to repeat our own career." [26] We have not understood that "the organs of political action" are determined by social and economic forces which are beyond human control.

But this insistence on the link between American ideals and material conditions must ultimately bring Turner face to face again with the fact that the unique conditions were gone, the frontier had vanished. America, in 1918, was different in material structure from the rural utopia of 1865. As Turner himself asserted: "The transformations through which the United States is passing in our own day are so profound, so far-reaching, that it is hardly an exaggeration to say that we are witnessing the birth of a new nation in America." [27] And in this new nation where "The familiar facts of the massing of population in the cities and the contemporaneous increase of urban power, and of the massing of capital and production in fewer and vastly greater industrial units, especially attest the revolution," [28] Turner was not able to give the American people any firm assurance that their escape from historical complexity to natural simplicity had not ended with the passing of their beloved frontier. Indeed, the logic of his own philosophy of determinism led inexorably to the conclusion that American democracy was doomed.

Turner had failed to find the intellectual formula to preserve the Jeffersonian covenant in the new urban-industrial society of late nineteenth-century America. If this tradition was to be preserved, a political philosopher must appear who could prove that the Jeffersonian covenant with primitivism and nature was compatible with progress and industrialism. This political philosopher was to be Charles A. Beard, a political scientist who became a historian to fulfill the metaphysical and theological requirements of defending the Jeffersonian covenant in the twentieth century.

4. CHARLES A. BEARD: INDUSTRIALISM AND THE COVENANT RESTORED

Between 1900 and 1917, Charles Beard brought the unresolved tensions of Turner's historical imagination into an apparently successful synthesis. The major ideological problem that Turner was unable to overcome was his belief that an alien business aristocracy and an alien proletariat were being introduced into the nation by the economic force of industrialism. The business aristocracy of 1830 could be destroyed because it was opposed by the dominant natural force of the early nineteenth century, the frontier. Now, however, the business aristocracy of 1890 seemed to be supported by industrialism, the dominant natural force of the late nineteenth century. But Charles Beard was to argue, and to persuade much of his generation, that industrialism as an impersonal force beyond human control must, therefore, be an instrument of progress. Industrialism was a force comparable to the physical frontier; it destroyed historical culture; it eroded institutions and traditions. If a complex social hierarchy existed in nineteenth-century America, it was not caused by industrialism as Turner believed. Indeed, Beard promised that industrialism would sweep away the plutocracy and proletariat of 1890.

And Beard could also synthesize Turner's continued commitment to world progress and Turner's ideological frustration that there was no way to share a disappearing physical frontier with mankind. If, as Beard argued, industrialism had the same progressive effect as the American frontier and if, on the other hand, industrialism could exist in every nation of the world, then it followed that industrialism, the new frontier, could liberate all nations from historical culture.

56

Born on the Indiana prairie, Beard was persuaded by 1894 while he attended DePauw College that the great cities that were transforming the Midwest were related to the force of industrialism which had begun in Europe. Convinced that he could understand Chicago by studying Berlin and London, he left America to go to the Old World. Here, he was sure, he could discover the future destiny of the United States. It was during the late 1890's, while living in Germany and England, that Beard became certain of the frontier qualities of industrialism. He saw its ability to destroy established institutions and traditions. He visualized its ability to create a heavenly city on earth. Quickly he ceased to be a student of European conditions and became a prophet and teacher for those Europeans who were not yet as aware as the young American of the benevolent nature of industrialism. After preaching and teaching in England from London across the Midlands to the North, Beard brought his message back home to America in book form as *The Industrial Revolution.*

Apparently breaking from the tradition of Bancroft and Turner, Beard found the salvation of man not in escape to nature but in escape from nature. "Man, who through the long centuries had toiled with his hands, aided by crude implements, to wrest a pitiful subsistence from nature, suddenly discovered that the blind forces against which he had been struggling could be chained to do his work. . . . Suddenly, almost like a thunderbolt from a clear sky, were ushered in the storm and stress of the Industrial Revolution. The mechanical inventions of the centuries were eclipsed in less than one hundred years." [1]

This fantastic economic change, he wrote, had brought about social chaos. The gift of mechanical efficiency turned England from a medieval society with "rigidity of structure and immutability of function" into a living hell as each individual savagely competed against every other individual in order to survive. And industrial progress had brought the cruel paradox of increased poverty. But this was only temporary. There was, Beard continued, a law of progress running through human history. The first part of this law was immediately apparent at the beginning of the industrial revolution: "the substitution of intelligence for precedent." The second part of the law only gradually emerged in nineteenth-century England: the substitution of "organization for chaos and anarchy."

Gradually, Englishmen became aware that the organic society of the medieval past, marked by unequal classes, need not be replaced by a society of free but competing individuals. There could be an organic and democratic society. The industrial revolution, by destroying feudal class structure, had made democracy, the rule of the people, possible. Slowly, inexorably, the people of England learned of this democratic possibility and asserted themselves. "Within the past one hundred years the world has witnessed a silent revolution in English politics, which has resulted in the vesting of power in the hands of the people." [2]

Turner had linked industrialism and the undemocratic institution of the corporation. It was the development of the corporation in the 1880's and 1890's with its organized army of employees, supervised and controlled by a hierarchy of officers, which seemed to end all hope of the preservation of the self-reliant and self-sufficient individual produced by the frontier experience. Beard, however, now claimed that the English experience demonstrated that industrialism did not mean an inevitable retreat into a feudal state dominated by the "robber barons" who controlled the corporations. In England, Beard argued, it has been proved that industrial life can be organized around the cooperative. Triumphantly he declared that industrialism was itself a frontier force destroying social and economic hierarchies. Joyfully he announced that Americans in 1900 stood on the threshold of a great new progressive movement because of the force of industrialism: "Just as the political history of the past one hundred years has centered in political democracy, so the industrial history . . . has centered in Industrial Democracy." [3] There seems "to be but little doubt that the trusts are merely pointing the way to higher forms of industrial methods in which the people, instead of a few capitalists, will reap the benefits." [4]

Beard found, however, that his United States in 1900 was not ready to be redeemed by a young citizen of the industrial world. Here there was not the same ferment as in England among either the intellectuals or labor. The yoke of myth still burdened the American imagination. Beard had to gain intellectual respectability and prestige in order to build a massive ideological attack upon the established outlook. In 1904, his dissertation for the doctorate in political science appeared; it was a completely noncontroversial study of *The Office of the Justice of the Peace in England*. It dealt with England before the industrial revolution; it had no contemporary message. But then he collaborated with a Columbia historian, James Harvey Robinson, to publish in 1907 a textbook called *The Development of Modern Europe*. It marked the beginning of his educational campaign for America.

In the preface, the authors argued that they had not written just another textbook. This was "new history." It differed from the established historical approach by focusing first on the present and then going back into the past in order to trace the development of the most significant factors that were operating in contemporary society. Beard and Robinson stated that they were going to put fresh emphasis on the eighteenth century because it was here and not in the nineteenth century that the twentieth century had its true historical roots. The eighteenth century, they continued, witnessed the dual revolution that began modern history. There was the economic upsurge of the industrial revolution and there was the intellectual upsurge of the Enlightenment. Together, these served to free Western man from the medieval past. The industrial revolution made progress possible and the intellectual revolution of the Enlightenment brought forth a self-conscious philosophy of progress. And the civilization of the twentieth century would be built on both the fact and the ideal of progress.

Progress, they wrote in tones reminiscent of Bancroft, was the escape from peasantry, from aristocracy, from monarchy, and, above all, from the Roman Catholic Church of the Middle Ages. They found their greatest heroes among the scientists of the Age of Enlightenment, who urged "that man was by nature good; that he should freely use his own God-given reason; that he was capable of becoming increasingly wise by a study of nature's laws, and that he could indefinitely better his own condition and that of his fellows if he would but free himself from the shackles of error and superstition." [5]

This outlook liberated France from the medieval past in the French Revolution. Unfortunately, wrote Beard and Robinson, the first and constructive part of this revolution was undermined by a second phase under the control of political fanatics whose irresponsibility had held back progress in France for half a century. Gradually, however, France began to move forward again toward Rousseau's ideal of government by all the people. Indeed, by 1850, there was evidence that democracy was moving ahead everywhere in western Europe. The spread of education, the use of the popular press, and the emancipation of women were making possible the creation of a unified and intelligent people who were able to govern themselves. It was true, the authors admitted, that industrialism had created many hardships in nineteenth-century Europe and, as a result, there arose the doctrines of Karl Marx who challenged the idea of peaceful progress. But Beard and Robinson rejected Marx. "It is clear . . . that the evils of our present organization are being more and more generally understood, and there is hope that many shocking inequalities may gradually be done away with." [6]

Progress is scientifically demonstrable and progress means the spread of democracy — such was Beard's fundamental faith in 1908. In this year, Beard gave a lecture entitled "Politics," which reveals in detail the synthesis he had made between his faith in democracy and his faith in science.

He began by calling attention to the fact that recently the study of political science has been forced to take history, economics, and sociology into account. Many, he said, believe that the study of politics therefore has ceased to be a science. But, for Beard, it seemed rather that finally "solid foundations are being laid in reality in place of the shifting sands of speculation. We are getting away from metaphysics, from artificialities, to find the whole man participating in the work of government." From the historians and the Darwinians, political scientists are learning that "man is infinite in variety and capacity" and that political history is not a decline from a state of nature but an upward movement out of "a dim and dateless past . . . into an illimitable future, which many of us believe will not be hideous and mean, but beautiful and magnificent." [7]

If history is progress, Beard argued, then the nineteenth-century political scientists who argued that the forms of nineteenth-century government and law were eternal and immutable must be mistaken. The absolute claims for freedom of contract and private property must be modified. Men would never achieve pure communism, Beard wrote, but neither could they live with pure *laissez-faire*. Let us then, he declared, escape from the class bias which makes us too defensive about contracts and property and see the facts as they really are.

We must remember, he continued, that the essence of political life is sovereignty. In the history of Western civilization, there has been a trend to take sovereignty from the king and place it with the people. And yet in the United States of America, Beard declared, we have not a democratic constitution but an aristocratic one, which balances one group against another; it is "inefficient for positive action . . . and characterized by that irresponsibility which power inevitably engenders." Compare this, he urged, with an ideal democratic society "where the rule of the majority is frankly recognized (a condition of affairs gravely feared by the framers of our Constitution), government tends toward a type, unified in internal structure, emancipated from formal limitations, and charged with direct responsibility to the source of power." [8]

Since the trend of history is toward democracy, since one can see the evolution of such political sovereignty of the people in England under the impact of industrialism, the United States, also experiencing the industrial revolution, must inevitably develop a democratic constitution, one which escapes from the aristocratic concept of checks and balances and frankly recognizes the rule of the majority. Advanced scholars, Beard pointed out, like Woodrow Wilson, Henry Jones Ford, and Frank Goodnow "have conclusively shown the unreality of the doctrine of divided powers, and the positive fashion in which our democratic political society seeks through extra-legal party organization to overcome the friction of a disjointed machine." [9]

Beard chose to end his lecture with a dramatic affirmation to his listeners that American industrial democracy was part of a worldwide pattern: A "new division of political research may be denominated world politics. . . . The shuttle of trade and intercourse flies ever faster and it may be weaving the web for a world state. It may be that steam and electricity are to achieve . . . that unity of mankind which rests on the expansion of a common consciousness of rights and wrongs through the extension of identical modes of economic activity." [10] Beard was promising the emancipation of the United States and the entire world from the bondage of historical institutions. He was pointing toward an imminent international millennium.

Beard had now developed the strategy of his philosophic campaign to force the American imagination from the bonds of the past so that industrial democracy might become a reality. He had to prove that the founding fathers were capitalistic aristocrats who feared and hated democracy and contrived a constitutional system designed to block the growth of democracy. While they had failed to stop the growth of democracy, their governmental pattern still existed to frustrate the will of the people. Beard had to prove to the American people that they owed no loyalty to a Constitution that had been deliberately constructed by aristocrats to keep the people out of power. The first blow of Beard's attack on the Constitution was struck with the publication in 1910 of his textbook *American Government and Politics.*

Here he announced to college freshmen that the American Revolution had not been fought in the name of democracy. The English colonies in

1775 were governed by an economic aristocracy which rebelled against England because of "discontent with economic restrictions, not with their fundamental political institutions." Certainly, he continued, they were "not motivated by the levelling doctrines with which the French middle class undermined the bulwarks of feudalism." [11]

Beard was repeating the traditional historical metaphysics of Bancroft and Turner. Like them, he assumed the existence of a democratic, classless society, the American people, in 1776 as well as the presence of an artificial, alien, English-oriented aristocracy. Like them, he defined this aristocracy as selfishly motivated and capable of using conspiracy to thwart the will of the people through institutional restraint.

Following Bancroft, Beard also assumed that the meaning of the Revolution transcended the motives of the aristocracy. The Revolution had become democratic and the people had expressed their ideal of freedom from the tyranny of history in the Declaration of Independence and the Articles of Confederation. But the founding fathers had struck back against such natural liberty and replaced it with the institutional power of the Constitution because "they had no quarrel with the system of class rule and the strong centralization of government which existed in England." [12] This was a selfish, grasping alien aristocracy who "were not seeking to realize any fine notions about democracy and equality. . . . They were anxious above everything else to safeguard the rights of property against any levelling tendencies." [13]

In 1912, Beard published a little book, *The Supreme Court and the Constitution*, which was a savage criticism of those of his fellow political scientists who were arguing that the attack of the contemporary Supreme Court on the social and economic legislation associated with the progressive movement was not in the tradition of the founding fathers. These men were asserting that the framers of the Constitution had not intended that the Supreme Court should block the will of the people by the use of the court's power of judicial review. Open your eyes, Beard almost shouted, and look at the facts. The Washingtons, Adamses, Madisons, Hamiltons, and Jays "regarded it as their chief duty, in drafting the new Constitution, to find a way of preventing the renewal of what they deemed 'legislative tyranny.' " [14]

During the 1780's, he continued, the colonial aristocracy had begun its counterrevolution against the popular democracy which had triumphed in 1776. "Under the Articles of Confederation populism had a free hand, for majorities in the state legislatures were omnipotent. Anyone who reads the economic history of the time will see why the solid conservative interests of the country were weary of talk about the 'rights of the people' and bent upon establishing firm guarantees for the rights of property." [15] The aristocrats saw in the doctrine of judicial review the best way of checking the will of the people. Again Beard drove home the un-American and exploitive ideology of the founding fathers: "judicial control was really a new and radical departure . . . which did not spring from Anglo-Saxon 'ideas' but from the practical necessity of creating a foil for the rights of property against belligerent democracy." [16]

The reasons for Beard's extreme hostility toward the founding fathers and their Constitution became perfectly clear in another of his textbooks, *Contemporary American History, 1877–1913*, published in 1914.

Our generation, he wrote, is characterized by economic revolution. We have become an industrial nation during these thirty years. And this material transformation must be accompanied by comparable changes in political and social thought, in legal and economic theory. This massive and necessary change in American civilization, however, has been made much more difficult by the fact that when the industrial revolution came to America from England, it brought with it English classical economic theory, the theory of *laissez-faire*, which has made impossible any real adjustment to the social and economic problems caused by industrialism. This fallacious economic philosophy was harmful enough in England but in America it took on disastrous proportions because here, unlike England, there was the Supreme Court of the United States to enforce this vicious economic theory. Worse still, the Supreme Court, which represented the reactionary tradition of the founding fathers, had acquired a potent new weapon to protect property from democracy, that clause in the Fourteenth Amendment to the Constitution which denied the states power over property.

From the Civil War until 1896, Beard continued, the American people had almost passively accepted the terrible problems of capitalism which threatened their democracy. Giant corporations, governed by an aristocratic elite, had arisen which denied the American creed of equality. And an industrial proletariat had developed which also denied the American creed of equality. Americans had passively accepted the growth of these problems because they refused to admit that new problems could occur in the United States after 1865. With the successful defense of national unity in the Civil War, Americans believed that perfection had been achieved. They believed that isolation from Europe saved them from the problems of that continent. They could not visualize industrialism as a force capable of bringing its problems from Europe to America. But there was, asserted Beard, an international frontier connected to industrialism which created common problems in every country.

If Americans would only look at England where industrialism was most advanced, however, they could take heart because they would see that industrialism was not just destructive. It made possible a new kind of democracy, an industrial democracy of social and economic planning. But if Americans were to engage in such social and economic planning, they must free their legislatures from judicial control. The sovereign will of the people must be free to express itself directly and completely through its legislative bodies.

In the election of 1896 Beard found evidence of a turning point in American history. The people were at last aroused to both the dangers and potentialities of the industrial revolution. From 1896 to 1912, the people were on the march to create a new democracy. They were striking down the power of the new captains of industry and their tools, the professional politicians, by establishing direct methods of expressing their will. There was new emphasis on direct elections, the initiative, the referendum, the recall, the popular election of United States senators; there was a demand to humble the new aristocracy by the use of an income tax.

This popular revolution brought a new emphasis on social and economic legislation that would check the growth of an American proletariat and lift the depressed masses back into the ranks of the people. Beard rejoiced that American provincialism was ended, that "it was apparent from an examination of the legislation of the first decade of the twentieth century that they [the United States] were well in the paths of nations like Germany, England, and Australia." [17]

Finally, the people had found in Theodore Roosevelt a leader for the new democracy. Roosevelt understood that industrialism had created a national economy which required control by the national government. He wanted a new democracy that was neither anarchic capitalism nor tyrannical socialism; he wanted a return to the middle way of the people, a philosophy of flexible utilitarianism which aimed to strengthen the democratic community. With deepest admiration, Beard quoted Roosevelt's formulation of this new democracy under the title "The New Nationalism": "The

New Nationalism puts the national need before sectional or personal advantages. It is impatient of the utter confusion that results from local legislatures attempting to treat national issues as local issues. It is still more impatient of the impotence which springs from overdivision of government powers, the impotence which makes it possible for local selfishness or for legal cunning, hired by wealthy special interests, to bring national activities to a deadlock. This New Nationalism regards the executive power as the steward of the public welfare. It demands of the judiciary that it shall be interested primarily in human welfare rather than in property, just as it demands that the representative body shall represent all the people." [18]

Beard had the sad task of ending his text with the report of a temporary setback of the new democracy that understood the industrial facts of life. By political accident, Roosevelt had been defeated in 1912 by Woodrow Wilson. Wilson was a professed Jeffersonian who refused to admit that America had become an urban-industrial civilization, a Jeffersonian who hoped to turn back toward the agricultural past. Wilson took this ridiculous stand because he defined the new industrialism in terms of trusts, which he called artificial entities. But Beard's readers were left with the impression that soon industrial democracy would surge forward again. Progress was inexorable; real democracy was inevitable.

It was within this context that Beard had built his major assault on that Constitution of the aristocrats, the Constitution of checks and balances which thwarted the will of the people. In 1913, he published *An Economic Interpretation of the Constitution of the United States*. This, the culmination of his effort to free the people from the legal shackles from the past, was the book that made Beard's reputation as a historian. From this moment on, most young men going into history looked, not to Turner, but to Beard as the intellectual leader of the profession.

This book clarified Beard's major quarrel with George Bancroft. While accepting the fundamental articles of the older historian's faith, Beard had to demonstrate that Bancroft had erred in his understanding of the Constitution. Bancroft had argued that the colonial aristocracy was directed by God to write a democratic constitution, just as it had been forced to lead a democratic revolution. For Bancroft, the only institutional power which the aristocracy exercised at the beginning of the nineteenth century was the Second Bank of the United States. When Jackson smashed the Bank, Bancroft had predicted the total and permanent disappearance of the colonial elite. Now Beard was to explain the continued existence and power of this un-American social class at the beginning of the twentieth century through its use of the institutional power of the Constitution and the Supreme Court. Beard was going to demonstrate that when the English-oriented aristocracy had written the Constitution, they were not inspired by God but only by their own greed.

If Beard could conclusively prove the economic selfishness of the founding fathers, he would break the chains of ideology which tied the loyalty of the people to the Constitution and the Court. When the people saw the truth that these were alien institutions used in the conspiracy of men pledged to impose European values upon America, they would rise up and smash these evil-doers and begin the millennium. This is the melodramatic ideological context for *The Economic Interpretation of the Constitution,* a book which presents a deceptively pedestrian and empirical façade.

Beard began his book with a plea for scholarly disinterestedness. Let us, he asked, test the hypothesis of economic interpretation as a way of understanding the writing of the Constitution. And, he added, it seems plausible to tentatively apply such an approach to the Constitution because the man who more than anyone else was responsible for the written form of the Constitution, James Madison, had urged that we understand history by the technique of economic interpretation.

If we accept Madison's theory, Beard continued, we must believe that historical change is the result of the clash of economic interests. At the beginning of the 1780's the states were leagued together as sovereign equals under the Articles of Confederation. By 1789, they were joined together as inferior units of a new nation, the United States of America. How does economic interest explain this great revolution? The crucial questions to ask, he concluded, are these: What economic groups wanted change? What economic groups wanted to preserve the *status quo*? What did the economic groups desiring change have to gain by the establishment of a new order? When we ask these questions, wrote Beard, we immediately discover that "Large and important groups of economic interests were adversely affected by the system of government under the Articles of Confederation, namely, those of public securities, shipping and manufacturing, money at interest; in short, capital as opposed to land. The representatives of these important interests attempted . . . to secure amendments to the Articles of Confederation which would safeguard their rights in the future. . . . Having failed to realize their great purposes through the regular means, the leaders in the movement set to work to secure by a circuitous route the assemblying of a convention to 'revise' the Articles of Confederation with the hope of obtaining, outside of the existing legal framework, the adoption of a revolutionary programme." [19]

Through brief biographies of all the members of the Constitutional Convention, Beard demonstrated to his own satisfaction that all the signers were related to the aggressive property interests he had described at the beginning of the book. He also argued that these men all shared the views expressed in *The Federalist Papers*. Here was class unity. "It is to the owners of personalty anxious to find a foil against the attacks of levelling democracy, that the authors of the Federalist address their most cogent arguments in favor of ratification." [20]

An awareness of Bancroft's metaphysics clarifies Beard's emphasis on the paper money interests of the founding fathers. For Bancroft, America was timeless reality because it was natural. Europe experienced the constant change of history because it was artificial, man-made. Beard was appealing to his readers' unconscious assumption of that distinction. If he could demonstrate that the monetary philosophy of the founding fathers was not rooted in nature but was committed to artificial values, he would be able to destroy their prestige. As Bancroft had stressed the artificial and materialistic aspect of the eastern aristocracy in its relation to the Second Bank of the United States, so Beard applied the same terms to the authors of the Constitution.

And as Bancroft had stressed the conspiracy of this group in its unsuccessful attempt to overthrow the rule of the "people" in the valley of democracy, so Beard stressed the use of conspiracy in replacing the Articles of Confederation with the Constitution. Since Beard, like Bancroft, assumed that the reality of America was a classless democracy, he must define aristocracy as alien and nonfunctional. He could not believe that there was any legitimate way for a colonial aristocracy to exercise leadership. By metaphysical conviction, Beard was forced to argue in the concluding chapters of his book that through trickery and subterfuge the Federalists overcame the will of the people and established the Constitution as the law of the land without popular support.

Having demonstrated that Bancroft was wrong in his analysis of the Constitution, Beard also had to persuade his contemporaries that Bancroft was wrong in arguing that progress was going to culminate in the agrarian commonwealth of Jefferson and Jackson. Because they were committed to that view, many Americans were not able to come to grips with the urban-industrial environment. Supporting Theodore Roosevelt's "New Nationalism" against Woodrow Wilson's "New Freedom," Beard had vehemently attacked Jefferson as the source of Wilson's philosophic weakness. Woodrow Wilson asks us to restore the national covenant of Jefferson, Beard wrote, but "agrarian democracy" is as fallacious "as the equally unreal and unattainable democracy of small business" that "is Wilson's goal." With great bitterness, Beard asked: "Today nearly half of us belong to the 'mobs of the great cities' — sores on the body politic. What message has the sage of Monticello for us?" [21]

To prove the inadequacy of Jefferson, Beard now published in 1915 *The Economic Origins of Jeffersonian Democracy*. Knowing that his audience believed in the values of a classless society of free and equal producers and that they assumed with Bancroft that Jefferson had been the prophet of such a democracy, Beard harshly separated Jefferson from the "people." Jefferson and his fellow Republican leaders were farmers, but unlike the "people," they formed "an aristocracy of slave-owning planters." They took power away from Hamilton, not because of their commitment to democracy, but to defend their own selfish, materialistic, and aristocratic interests.[22]

In 1915, Beard was pleading with Americans to concentrate on industrial America. Nostalgia for the past would only obscure the opportunity to take advantage of the freedom being created by the industrial frontier as it leveled the restrictive power of the eastern aristocracy. During this period of his greatest creative energy, he had also published two textbooks, *American Citizenship* and *American City Government*, to provide guidelines by which his generation could come to grips with the new kind of government activity needed in the new industrial age. Rejecting the *laissez-faire* doctrine of Bancroft, Beard wrote, ". . . the purpose of government . . . is to do those things which cannot be done well or justly by individuals working alone, and to regulate the doings of private persons in such a manner as to improve the general standard of life, labor, and education. The very essence of government, according to the democratic ideal, is cooperation or union of effort for the common good." [23] Summoning still further reserves of strength and inspiration, he joined the New York Bureau of Municipal Research and served as the director of its training school for public service.

In 1917, Beard believed with all his heart that he was participating in the first stages of a new democracy made possible by the industrial frontier. In the United States, across the face of the entire world, industrialism was smashing the institutional and traditional vestiges of historical civilization. Mankind everywhere was being emancipated from the slavery of history to live in the freedom of natural harmony. Behold, he declared, the victory of women in the United States who are at last winning the right to vote; this is "not . . . a temporary episode of current politics, but . . . a part of an age-long battle of the common mass of people upward from serfdom to freedom." [24] Look, he continued, at our young men; they too have emancipated themselves from the artificial culture of the nineteenth century and are addressing themselves to the new society in a series of liberal magazines, the *New Republic*, the *Nation*, and the *Dial*. The future was bright. The only dark cloud on the horizon was World War I. And Beard found that it had a most significant silver lining. There is a most important parallel between Beard's enthusiasm for the problem-solving possibilities of war and Bancroft's acceptance of the Civil War.

For Bancroft, the "people" were not able to deal with the problem of slavery between 1830 and 1860 because the use of politics to solve an institutional problem would involve Americans with planning, power, and complexity. By 1860, however, the alien and artificial southern aristocracy had conspired to destroy democracy. The "people" had then defended themselves by expressing their general will through the agency of the representative hero Abraham Lincoln. Pressured into a war against aggression, the "people" had used the force of war to simplify, to purge, to purify the country by destroying the institution of slavery and the institution of the southern aristocracy. They had restored the covenant of nature. For Bancroft, the people could be corrupted by the use of political power. They would not, however, lose their innocence in the use of the purgative force of war.

For Bancroft the natural frontier had inexplicably failed to destroy all complexity, leaving the southern aristocracy and its feudal institutions to exist in America; for Beard the industrial frontier had inexplicably failed to destroy the German aristocracy and its feudal institutions. As Bancroft had argued that aristocracy must always conspire to destroy democracy, so in 1917 Beard found the German Junkers conspiring to destroy democracy. And as Bancroft had rejoiced in being able to add the force of war to the force of the physical frontier as a means of destroying historical complexity, so Beard now rejoiced in the force of war added to the force of the industrial frontier as a means of destroying historical complexity. Germany was the only industrial nation where medieval institutions were still in existence. American participation in the war would ensure the destruction of the Kaiser and the Junkers. And then the world would be safe for democracy as America had become safe for democracy with the destruction of the southern aristocracy. War was morally preferable to political planning for Bancroft and Beard.

In a book, *National Governments and the World War,* published in 1919, Beard revealed the depth and intensity of his commitment to the final triumph of democracy at Armaggedon. "For more than two hundred years a great ideal has been taking form and spreading throughout the earth: governments must derive their powers from the consent of the governed. . . . The democratic principle has been compelled to battle every step of the long way from despotism to liberty against the ancient doctrine that government belongs by divine right to kings whom it is the duty of the people to obey in all things." [25] In Germany, alone of all the industrial nations, this medieval doctrine persisted and conspired to defeat democracy. The aggressive German aristocracy, proclaimed Beard, had forced war upon the peaceful United States. The American people resisted this brutal attack by expressing the power of their general will through the representative hero Woodrow Wilson. But Wilson was the representative hero of all the democratic peoples of the world including the German people. Wilson waged war only against the Kaiser and his war machine. He fought to liberate the German people from their tyrannical leaders. He would welcome them as equals in the concert of democratic nations who would compose a league to preserve the peace. In Woodrow Wilson, the people of the world had found their spokesman. His views reflected "the slowly maturing opinion of the masses of the people everywhere in the earth . . . those who have the faith will believe that a real change has come in the long course of history and that the years, 1917–1918, as surely as the age of the American and French Revolutions, will mark the opening of a new epoch in the rise of government by the people and in the growth of a concert among the nations." [26]

History as progress had reached final fulfillment in a state of natural simplicity for Beard in 1919 as it had for Bancroft in 1865. Beard's millennium, however, had one great advantage over that of his predecessor. Since Bancroft's Eden was for Americans only there was always the possibility that European corruption could again challenge the sanctity of the national covenant. There was always the possibility of further drama. But for Beard the entire world had been made safe for democracy. This was indeed the end of history and the culmination of progress; all the complexity of institutions and traditions had been swept away. Never again would the American national covenant be challenged because it had become the covenant of all the world.

It was with mounting horror, even terror, therefore, that Charles Beard surveyed the world of 1919. Cooperative democracy had not triumphed in the United States, where partisan politics reached new levels of bitterness. And the European countries were also racked with comparable partisan divisions to which was added national rivalry as each scrambled to expand boundaries at the expense of old and new neighbors. Competitive anarchy was the order of the day. How would Charles Beard react to the collapse of his vision of progress?

In 1919, the millennium had failed to arrive in the United States or in Europe. But, for Beard, there was a major difference in the situations of the New and Old worlds. He had believed that industrialism was going to destroy historical complexity and liberate Europeans to live in natural harmony. Now, however, Beard asked whether Europeans, who were by definition part of historical culture, could be made into "people" even by an industrial frontier. Perhaps industrialism could only restore natural democracy, not create it. Bancroft had limited the omnipotence of God to save Europeans; now Beard limited the saving grace of industrialism. As Beard retreated to isolation, the national covenant with nature became all important in his thinking. It must be preserved.

The first evidence of Beard's retreat to the Jeffersonian covenant is in a high school textbook he also published in 1919 in conjunction with William Bagley. Immediately, he struck the theme of Bancroft as he informed his youthful readers that humble Europeans had become Americans when they stepped out of the bondage of the feudal past and took on the characteristics of the yeoman farmer; he reversed his previous attitude toward Jefferson to describe him now as the incisive prophet of our agrarian democracy. "As Jefferson said, the man who owns his own land and looks to the sun in heaven and to the labor of his own hands for his sustenance, can have the spirit of independence which is the life breath of republics." [27]

In this textbook, Beard wrote, he would describe the life of the common people who are the basis of our democracy, the people who had emerged with the expansion of the midwestern frontier. With loving care, he described the details of pioneer life: of cabin building, of primitive farming, of the tasks of father, mother, and children. He was far from his vision of an international frontier of industrial democracy when he wrote: "The farmer, secure in the possession of his land and home, could snap his fingers at the world, knowing that the doings of kings, principalities, and the powers of Europe, or the course of events beyond the Alleghenies, could not deprive him of his daily bread. There was a genuine equality of people based on similarity of occupation and opportunity, and there was a spirit of liberty unique in our history. Each family was, in fact, almost entirely independent of the outside world." [28]

Almost word for word, Beard was echoing Bancroft and Turner. The machine was described to the students, not in the earlier Beard's terms as the liberator of all mankind, but in Turner's terms as the destroyer of the American Garden of Eden. "The great inventions created here [in America], as in Europe, millions of industrial workers and city dwellers and so brought to this country the same problems. One can truly say that the steam engine makes the whole world kin." [29] In 1919, Beard found, the whole world was kin in the common misery brought by the machine. And no people had lost as much as the Americans; they had lost the perfection of midwestern agrarian democracy. In a chapter on the triumph of industry, he recounted the numberless evils it had brought to the United States: poverty, slaves, child labor, the exploitation of women, financial panics, the waste of natural resources, and the massive combinations of capital and labor which threatened our tradition of individualism.

Nor could Beard completely reassure his readers in the subsequent chapter, "The New Democracy," that the people were rising to the challenge of the industrial revolution. Somehow his discussion of the Australian ballot or even women's suffrage did not equal in power his descriptions of industrial evils. Beard's only solution for these evils was that the people must stop working for their own selfish interests and dedicate themselves to the national interest. But he could no longer promise the immediate coming of the democratic millennium. Beard was on the defensive when he brought the book to a conclusion with a brief discussion of American entry into World War I in which he stressed that the United States had only defended itself against aggressive German militarism rather than forged a crusade to make the world safe for democracy.

When Beard abandoned his role as the prophet of a new international democracy, he became a Jeremiah who had the responsibility of calling his people back to the Jeffersonian covenant. His was the responsibility of calling attention to the evil, masquerading as the good, which threatened to undermine American innocence by linking the nation to the corruption of Europe. No one knew this evil better than Beard—it was the philosophy of internationalism. Boldly, he struck out at this weakness in 1922 with *Cross Currents in Europe To-day*. Intellectuals had become converted to internationalism because they had looked too narrowly at the economic facts of American life. They had seen the great involvement of the nation in the world economy from the beginning of the colonies until 1914, an involvement which had forced Americans to participate in every major European war. They now were faced with the even greater participation of the United States in foreign trade. During the war, the exports of agricultural and industrial goods had increased and had been joined by the export of capital. The intellectuals were right. "The world is an economic unit and the United States is being woven into the very fabric of that unity." [30]

The assumption of the intellectuals was that the basis of the world economy was to be the peaceful, cooperative force of industrialism. But, Beard cried out, look at the revelations that have come out of the official archives of Russia, Germany, and Austria. We intellectuals believed the war was caused by feudalism. Now we discover that it was the result of capitalism. And "If the last World War grew mainly out of commercial rivalry . . . and if we now see signs of a more intense rivalry than ever supported by all the powerful agencies of government, what then shall we say of the future?" [31]

The answer, for Beard, was inexorable. When feudalism died in Europe, it was not replaced by the peaceful force of industrialism but by the warlike force of capitalism. Aggressive capitalism would inevitably bring World War II unless the United States came to Europe and exerted powerful leadership to end the commercial rivalry of the European states and lead the European nations into political union and cooperation. But Beard, like Bancroft and Turner, was committed to an ideology which denied the possibility of creative political leadership. Innocence and power were incompatible. The impersonal force of industrialism had failed to create the basis of democracy in Europe. Men could not hope to accomplish what the impersonal forces of history had failed to achieve. Americans had only one choice: to preserve their own democracy and avoid the next war that must come to Europe. The logical implications of Beard's argument were complete political and economic isolation from Europe.

Beard, the Jeremiah, asked what would happen if the intellectuals of America did not repent their internationalism? In a peaceful America, rooted in the cooperativeness of agricultural and industrial democracy, the source of all discord was located among the great financial capitalists of the eastern cities. It was these men who preached the English doctrine of ruthless competition at home and abroad. If the intellectuals continued a policy of internationalism, they would increase the ideological and economic strength of the financial capitalists; they would keep the door open for the influx of foreign ideology, and the financiers would gain economic strength from the export of capital abroad. This was imperialism; it would commit the government to the protection of this foreign investment and soon the nation would be involved in the same commercial rivalry which had caused American participation in World War I and which would lead us inexorably into World War II.

Because the American past was one of agricultural democracy not feudalism, Beard declared, industrialism would re-create in the United States the pattern of a modern cooperative and democratic society comparable to that of 1800. The task of the intellectual was first to see that eastern capitalism did not corrupt this natural democracy. But, more important, the intellectual must help to destroy this artificial and un-American financial aristocracy. The intellectual had this power because it did not involve the creation of the real bases of society; this democracy had been constructed by the impersonal forces of the agrarian frontier and then reconstructed by industrialism. The freedom of the intellectual was to be fulfilled through the disestablishment of the parasitical and artificial ways of financial capitalism which were in conflict with these real and productive forces.

This was the theme that Beard hammered home in his *Economic Basis of Politics*. He would dramatize for American intellectuals the bankruptcy of European democratic ideology symbolized by Rousseau. Rousseau, Beard admonished, was the typically impractical European philosopher who prophesied the worldwide triumph of democracy without consideration for the necessary economic base for democratic development. Against this otherworldly dreamer Beard contrasted the practical realism of James Madison. Here was the ideal type of American political philosopher who refused to speculate but rather looked at the brute facts as they existed. It was Madison who argued the possibility of the American democratic experiment because the nation's economic pattern rested upon the freehold farm.[32]

Beard, striking a pose as the nation's Jeremiah, in the middle of the 1920's, wrapped himself in mantles of Jefferson the idealist and Madison the realist. The United States, he preached, still possessed the national covenant of Jefferson. And if, in rededicating our loyalty to Jefferson, we recognized that this covenant depended upon a favorable economic foundation, if we accepted the realism of Madison, then Americans would have both the spiritual and intellectual strength to meet the continuing challenge of the conspiratorial eastern aristocracy and to go forward to destroy this enemy and restore the national covenant to pristine purity and preserve the people in their perfect innocence. This Jeremiad was to form the basis of Beard's historical writings until the defeat of his policy of isolation at the end of the 1930's.

Not all of Beard's contemporaries, however, were able to retreat to the Jeffersonian covenant after World War I shattered their dream of an international millennium. Such a historian of the "lost generation" was Carl Becker.

5 CARL BECKER: EUROPE AND THE ROOTS OF THE COVENANT

THE FAITH and philosophy which underlie the historical writings of Frederick Jackson Turner and Charles A. Beard are revealed in full clarity in the magnificently lucid prose of Carl Becker, Turner's student and Beard's contemporary as a spokesman for history as progress.

This was an unusual destiny for a youth who had been born on an Iowa farm in 1873 and reared in Waterloo, Iowa, by a father who had come west to seek his fortune and had found it as a successful farmer and town builder. The elder Becker, a pillar of the Republican party and the Methodist Church, expected his son to take his place as a member of this prosperous agricultural society. But Carl Becker dreamed of becoming a scientist or a novelist. Having made an intellectual break with his family before he entered the University of Wisconsin, he was free to be attracted by the exceptional teaching of Turner and to be led toward the profession of history, a career choice which shocked his father as much as his previous interest in science or writing.

During his college years at Wisconsin, there was a continued, steady, and quiet rebellion against his childhood background. Personally shy and retiring, Becker was committed to an intellectual questioning of the established order. In his undergraduate notebook, there is recorded his growing doubt about the Methodist orthodoxy of his youth; soon he would also begin to question the Republicanism of his past. Frederick Jackson Turner recognized the unusual qualities of the young Becker; here was someone who could analyze and who could write. He and other teachers encouraged Becker to go east to stretch his imagination by contact with the interpretations of other historians.

When Becker left for Columbia University, there is no doubt that he carried a great intellectual legacy from Turner. He was persuaded of the importance of the frontier thesis; he was sure also that frontier democracy was threatened by new industrial America. He had Turner's faith that historians could illuminate the present crisis, that history had practical importance. He believed with Turner that there needed to be much more emphasis on economic history and that historians must borrow from the other social sciences as they performed the practical task of delineating the economic revolution.

At Columbia, he enrolled in a seminar in eighteenth-century thought given by James Harvey Robinson, who was to become the father of the "new history." Actually, the "new history" preached by Robinson was very close to Turner's emphasis on the practicality of historical research. In Robinson, then, Becker found a kindred spirit who sympathized with the young Iowan's view that "to me nothing can be duller than historical facts, and nothing more interesting than the service they can be made to render in the effort to solve the everlasting riddle of human experience." [1] Clearly, Becker's lasting interest in the intellectual history of the eighteenth century also developed in Robinson's class. And his concern for relating American thought to European civilization may well have been stimulated by his contact with Robinson. The seeds for a break with Turner may have been sown. Turner's frontier thesis stressed the uniqueness of America. Becker learned from Robinson the intimate relationship of American ideals to the Enlightenment. Ultimately, he would try to place America within the context of the European past. But not yet.

In a course on colonial America given by Herbert Osgood, Becker began the dissertation he would finish back at Wisconsin: *The History of Political Parties in the Province of New York, 1760–1776.* The central idea of this study echoed Turner's belief that the Revolution had a double meaning. As Becker phrased this view: "The American Revolution was the result of two general movements; the contest for home-rule and independence, and the democratization of American politics and society. Of these movements, the latter was fundamental; it began before the contest for home-rule, and was not completed until after the achievement of independence." [2] Becker wrote that the revolutionary crisis grew out of the constitutional issue of whether the colonies should continue to operate under the principles of representative government or be subjected more and more to monarchical control from England. In New York, the Assembly worked to preserve its power against the aggressions of the governor who represented the royal authority of England. During the decade from 1765 to 1775, the privileged class of colonial aristocrats was forced to ask the disfranchised people for help in its struggle to stop the growth of royal authority. Ultimately, the aristocrats in the assembly felt the necessity to create extralegal political machinery in the forms of committees and congresses to fight English policy. To justify these procedures, they appealed to the principles of the natural rights of all men. This theory and practice fostered the growth of democratic ideology and democratic participation in New York politics. Soon the crisis with England reached a point of no return; colonial leaders must either submit to English authority or become open revolutionists fighting for independence. Now, Becker argued, the political presence of the people made the crucial difference in New York by forcing most of the colonial aristocrats to choose revolution. The common people, who had been recruited by the aristocrats to support their anti-English policy, were now determined to go on to independence. If the conservatives refused to give leadership to the Revolution, they might lose everything, including their property. If they assumed leadership, they might be able to preserve the existing political and economic structure of the colony. And this was what they did. But Becker made it clear that the days of aristocratic control were numbered. When the people found a leader, a Jefferson, then America would enter the nineteenth century destined to become a democratic nation.

Published in 1909, Becker's thesis was the first carefully documented study of the existence of class struggle in America at the time of the Revolution, the peculiar American class struggle of the "people" against an artificial, un-American aristocracy. It made Becker's reputation as a leading American historian. This was the era of the progressive movement when it was the responsibility of the people once more to throw off the rule of an artificial un-American aristocracy. Here was that substantial evidence, sought by Beard, that the Constitution, used by the modern aristocracy to block the will of the people, had been the creation of a colonial aristocracy which also had been anxious to frustrate the common man.

But Becker's central philosophical concern, unlike Beard's, was not to demonstrate that the founding fathers were aristocratic and un-American. Becker believed that his fellow historians had the responsibility of leading the people out of institutional bondage to the eastern plutocracy. He was aware, however, that his colleagues in the historical profession were embarrassed about any participation in a political movement, even a democratic one. From the moment when the historical profession had been established in the 1880's, historians had defined themselves as scientists who must studiously remove themselves from public life if they were to achieve objectivity. Becker was to leave the rewriting of the historical record to men like Beard, therefore, because he believed that his major intellectual responsibility was in the field of historiography, that he had the duty to demonstrate to his fellow historians that they could not escape participation in the political values of their society. It was useless, in Becker's view, to reveal the danger to the national covenant if historians did not believe they had both the freedom and the responsibility to act in its defense. This was the other part of Becker's educational task. It was not enough for him to argue that historians could never wall themselves within an ivory tower; he must also prove that all the people, including historians, had the creative freedom to shape the course of history. He must prove that his great teacher Frederick Jackson Turner was in error when he accepted the German philosophy of historical inevitability. This then was how Becker defined his greatest personal contribution to progressivism — the liberation of his colleagues from the chains of German historiography so that they could participate in the progressive movement and help destroy the threat of the eastern oligarchy to introduce institutional complexity that could undermine the Jeffersonian covenant with nature.

In an essay of 1910 entitled "Detachment and the Writing of History," Becker began the philosophical reorientation of his colleagues by quoting a critic who had found recent historical writing useless for any understanding of the world in which men live. According to this critic, historians were content to establish the validity of particular facts and to gather these verified facts together in helter-skelter fashion, letting the reader attempt to find meaningful patterns. Becker agreed with the critic's analysis. My colleagues' creed, he wrote, is that the historian is not to generalize. "History is what happened; the historian must write it down . . . *wie es ist eigentlich gewesen.*" [3] Why, Becker asked, have my colleagues taken this position? If it is because they believe that they can escape from the responsibility of judgment by arguing that the historical fact is purely objective, Becker continued, they are wrong. One cannot talk about a historical fact without relating it to another. And this inevitable relationship is supplied by the historian's mind. The relationships that historians make arise from their own social experience. "The historian cannot separate himself from the process he describes."

Each generation necessarily writes history according to its interests and needs, he continued. Within each generation, there is an area of agreement among the various historians because they are part of their society and reflect its outlook. The most recent generation of historians had agreed that history served no function, that history had no meaning, because their society defined no problems that needed to be solved. But now "In an age when industrial problems are pressing for solution the 'economic interpretation of history' is the thing." Becker made it clear that historians were now defining problems and using history to solve them because their society had become committed to problem-solving. The role of scientific, detached historians who were neutral toward their subject matter was not functional to a period when people had to grapple with enormous economic change. Morally committed historians, Becker predicted, inevitably would replace those of the uncommitted school.

Becker, however, in arguing the social role and responsibility of historians, was not breaking from the tradition of Bancroft and Turner and the Jeffersonian covenant. What Becker was trying to establish was that the world of big business and the corporation was artificial and alien to the authentic American experience of harmony with physical nature. Like Beard, he was criticizing Turner for identifying English business culture with the industrial process. Like Beard, Becker believed that industrialism was an impersonal and natural economic process which necessarily encouraged the same type of cooperative democracy which these two historians associated with the homestead farm of the Jeffersonian republic and which, therefore, was inimical to the parasitical and artificial patterns of business organization.

For Becker, as for Beard, it was inevitable that industrialism would destroy the robber barons and their undemocratic corporations. The free will which he urged upon his colleagues was that of George Bancroft; it was the freedom to disestablish the vestiges of European culture in America; it was the freedom to defend the covenant with nature. Becker, in 1910, unlike his teacher Turner, was able to see the Populism of the Great Plains, not as a last protest against an alien order which inexorably was destroying the Jeffersonian covenant, but as a model for the democratic commonwealth which was going to reappear in the East when the implacable force industrialism, speeded by a progressive rebellion of the people, destroyed this modern conspiracy of the eastern aristocracy against American democratic uniqueness.

In another essay of 1910, "Kansas," Becker begged his fellow historians to plunge into the tide of progress without fear because it was destined to carry them back to primitive democratic simplicity, which still existed in Kansas, a state "that is more Puritan than the New England of today." There, he continued, "Americanism, pure and undefiled, has a new lease on life. It is the mission of this self-selected people to see that it does not perish from off the earth." [4] Here, he declared, can still be found the way of life of the Jeffersonian republic before English capitalism in conjunction with the eastern aristocracy had begun to obscure American natural reality with the artificial and alien patterns of business culture.

By 1913, there was no evidence of historical relativity in Becker's writing. He had placed historians within culture and he had placed culture in motion but that motion was channeled in only one direction — that of progress. Just as George Bancroft had created a complex, artificial, and alien class structure in America between 1800 and 1830 so that he could proclaim a progressive movement that would restore Jeffersonian simplicity, Becker had now done the same for the years 1880–1910. And like Bancroft, Becker would try to rally his nation's intellectuals to participate in this progressive crusade that would re-establish a primitive perfection.

The climax of his scholarly call to arms came in 1913 with his essay, "Some Aspects of the Influence of Social Problems and Ideas upon the Study and Writing of History." With precision and eloquence, he moved through those areas of the philosophy of history with which he had been struggling for the last several years. He began with the assertion that every historian selects material; the facts do not speak for themselves; they speak to and through historians. But the individual historian makes selections which are meaningful to other historians and to the general public. He does this because he views the past through the eyes of his society and relates the past to the most pressing problems of his society. But in recognizing his essentially social role, Becker declared, the historian should not feel that he has lost the right to be called a scientist. The philosophy of John Dewey, he continued, has demonstrated that the only meaningful definition of intelligence is that it is an instrument that men use pragmatically to adjust to the facts of an unknown world. Intellectual activity, under this definition, has scientific validity only when it solves the problems of society. If this is true, Becker affirmed, then history can only be scientific when it serves as an instrument of community life. And conversely, those who hold to the Germanic theory of scientific neutrality are proved to be utterly unscientific. It is these misguided historians who are truly the prisoners of irrational myth and not those who write history which will help their community make progress.

After all, Becker wrote, the so-called scientific history of the nineteenth century was not really based on a conviction of the intrinsic worth of objective neutrality; it represented an emotional reaction against doctrines of 1789. In the early nineteenth century, conservatives turned to history to provide security against the liberating doctrines of the French Revolution. In the idealistic philosophy of Hegel, they found the perfect conservative doctrine which denied that men could find values outside the immediate historical context and declared that men must accept their society and wait for it to progress by principles which are inherent within it and which work without individual effort. In the middle of the nineteenth century, he pointed out, idealistic history gave way to scientific history without any major change in essential meaning. Again the individual had to wait for progress to happen to him under the influence of forces beyond his control.

Now, Becker continued, we are aware that during the last twenty years we have experienced "a revival of faith in the possibility of social regeneration, a revival, one might almost say, of the optimistic spirit of the eighteenth century." This is a renewed faith in democracy and the capacity of science to serve democracy, "the belief that society can, by taking thought, modify the conditions of life, and thereby indefinitely improve the happiness and welfare of all men." Historians must serve this faith and turn away from the "barren scholasticism" which has marked their efforts. They must "appropriate out of the past something which may serve that ideal of social progress which is the sum and substance of our modern faith." [5]

For a decade, Becker had urged Americans to think of themselves as actors in the drama of history who shaped their social environment under the inspiration of faith and will; he had urged them to reject the philosophy that man has no control over his society. But Becker no more than his mentor, Turner, believed that man had the freedom to create the good society. Kansans had democracy because they had escaped from eastern complexity to the simplicity of nature. Other Americans would have democracy in the twentieth century because industrialism would destroy the complexity of the eastern business empires. Becker was really urging Americans to have the will to destroy the artificial business society which had obscured the old agrarian democracy and which now prevented the appearance of a new industrial democracy. Becker was asking Americans to have faith in a law of progress that would inevitably destroy the complexity and evil of their current business-dominated society. He was calling on them to join in a crusade which would accelerate the course of progress. But the people did not create the ultimate pattern of progress; their creativity was limited to the destruction of the old order. Their faith and will was guaranteed by the fact of progress.

Many interpreters of Becker have found him to be a man of acute intelligence but without a deep range of emotional experience. Such an interpretation ignores the almost unbearable intellectual and emotional experience of Carl Becker during his years in Kansas. Becker had come to teach at the University of Kansas with the faith that here, if anywhere, pure agrarian democracy existed, that here was the democratic model for all men to pattern themselves after as they escaped from history. But after a decade of living in Kansas and teaching in one of the midwestern state universities that Turner visualized as the citadel of democratic ideals, Becker was disillusioned. In 1916, when he left the University of Kansas, Becker was a disenchanted agrarian. Bitterly he explained in his letters of resignation that Kansas lacked leadership; the narrow-minded businessmen who ran the state also dominated the university and hindered its academic development. He sought refuge at Cornell University. Here, in the physical isolation of Ithaca, no one asked him to lead a crusade to make history the guide to the progressive utopia nor did he have the responsibility of defending midwestern democracy. Here Becker could begin a grand retreat to the nineteenth-century role for the historian, that of the neutral observer.[6]

The first evidence of the great intellectual and emotional agony that must have gone into Becker's disillusionment is revealed in 1915. With apparent calm, he reversed the passionate hopes of a decade of crusading intellectual effort in a book review of L. Cecil Jones's *The Interpretation of History*. Jones's major thesis, Becker wrote, was that history must provide a clue to the future. With cool restraint, Becker rejected this idea. Speaking directly to Jones's utilitarian hypothesis, he wrote, "This is, I think, a fundamental error, and one which springs from a vicious confusion of the physical and moral world." [7] In the philosophy of the frontier and in the philosophy of the Enlightenment, Becker had seen a fruitful association of nature and morality. Now he damned this view as vicious. We must listen closely to his words because he is cutting his ties with the first forty years of his life so quietly that one who is not sharply attentive may miss the sound of the crashing down of the American dream. He wrote in 1915 as if he had always advised stoic acceptance by men of their fate: "The value of history is, indeed, not scientific but moral: by liberalizing the mind, by deepening the sympathies, by fortifying the will, it enables us to control, not society, but ourselves — a much more important thing; it prepares us to live humanely in the present and to meet rather than to foretell the future." [8]

Perhaps Becker tried to gain the strength to meet this bleak future through the example of his beloved *philosophes*. From his seminar with Robinson, he had come to share their faith; now he had to learn to live with their pessimism. When Becker arrived in Kansas, he was asked to teach European history; from 1902 to 1914, his reading was basically in this area. Now, in 1915, he was to publish his first essay in European intellectual history. In a second life after forty, Becker was to gain a reputation as a leading scholar and producer of scholars in the area of the French Enlightenment and the French Revolution. The move from the committed world of Kansas to the uncommitted atmosphere of Cornell may have been accidental and its symbolism may be erroneous but there is nothing accidental about the move Becker made from the essay on Kansas in 1910 to that on "The Dilemma of Diderot" in 1915. Nothing less than an intellectual and emotional revolution is involved.

The new Becker wrote with a gentle irony about an eighteenth-century intellectual who had believed in reform and had worked to bring it about. Diderot had hated the established religion and philosophy of his day because he believed these traditions encouraged immorality. He had insisted that they be replaced with a "new metaphysics and a new religion, a metaphysics rationally defensible and a religion morally sound." To destroy the old and enthrone the new, Diderot used the arguments of science. Men, he wrote, should believe only that which they can verify by the scientific method. We can know only specific, concrete facts, Diderot insisted, and, therefore, no man can successfully demonstrate the nonempirical values of the *ancien regime*.

But here, Becker wrote, was the dilemma which caused Diderot to stop publishing his writings at the peak of his intellectual power. Honest man that he was, Diderot, after the first flush of his attack on his enemies, had come to ask himself what morality could be established on the authority of a scientific position of materialism and empiricism. After all, if man is not shaped by spiritual forces, if he does not have a permanent nature, if, indeed, he is merely one material object in a world of many concrete, specific objects — all without inherent value — then how can man define what morality is? Human life, as part of physical nature, shares the neutral aspects of nature. Human life can be described by the scientific method, but it cannot be so judged.

What was Diderot to do? He believed that man knew only what science told him and yet science was not able to teach man what was moral. The philosophy of science of the Enlightenment, judged by Diderot's pragmatic test that it must produce more good men than established religion had done, quite clearly had failed. Diderot was faced with the appalling fact that "The identification of man and nature, and the conception of both as the necessary product of uniform natural law, had done nothing more after all than to put blind force in the place of God, and by eliminating purpose from the world leave men face to face with the *reductio ad absurdum* that 'whatever is is right.' " [9] And so was Becker faced with this fact.

Diderot's dilemma was meaningful only to one whose faith in progress needed to be reinforced by empirical verification, to one who, like Carl Becker, now found facts to be in conflict with faith. It was the nineteenth century, not the eighteenth, Becker had written again and again before 1915, which believed that "whatever is is right." Always before 1915, he had found the men of the Enlightenment to be men of faith. Now he focused on one *philosophe* who was deficient in faith, who must have his faith reinforced by science, and who failed to find that help. Carl Becker had made a pilgrimage back to the source of his belief in progress to restore his faltering faith; instead he found only despair.

The participation of the United States in World War I momentarily reversed Becker's growing pessimism. The enthusiasm for a war to make the world safe for democracy, to spread democracy everywhere, swept Becker out of the isolation of Cornell and restored his vision of the second coming of the Enlightenment.

In May of 1917, Becker published an article, "The Monroe Doctrine and the War," in the *Minnesota History Bulletin.* Its purpose was to convince his friends in the Midwest to surrender their tradition of isolation. Yes, wrote Becker, April 1917 marks a revolution in American history: Americans have broken from the principles of the Monroe Doctrine. From Washington to Wilson, Americans had believed that the United States must stay away from European politics if its democratic experiment was to have a fair chance to succeed or fail on its own merits or weaknesses. Our isolation was for the benefit of the world because if the experiment succeeded here, it could become the model for the peoples in other countries. Now the time has come, Becker continued, for our democratic generosity to take another shape. The war in Europe is a struggle between the democratic ideals that have been growing for a century in the Old World in spite of the continued existence of aristocratic and military ideals from out of the past. If German aristocracy wins, he warned, not only will European democracy be destroyed but American democracy will be threatened. If the United States fights and destroys the aristocracy of Germany, it will be making democracy secure in the world. The Monroe Doctrine was a means to that end. Now a new means to achieve that end is needed. American entry into the war was not, therefore, a revolution in ideals but only a change in means.[10]

Becker went on to Washington to join George Creel's Committee on Public Information and to share in the bitter outpouring of hatred for the German leaders. Here he wrote that "the Germans instituted in Belgium a reign of terror such as has not been known among civilized nations. . . . The record of senseless crimes and cruelties, of bestial acts, of nameless obscenities and revolting savagery which must be charged to the account of the German army in Belgium recalls those deeds by which 'The Huns, under their king Attila, a thousand years ago, made a name for themselves which is still mighty in tradition and story.' " [11] This was the evil in the world and it was being destroyed. When the German aristocracy was obliterated from the face of the earth, then good would triumph and democracy would flourish. In another pamphlet on *America's War Aims and Peace Program*,[12] Becker dramatized the revolutionary nature of President Wilson's vision of a new international order of free and equal democratic nations cooperating in a league of peace.

In 1918, Becker published a volume which reflected his renewed democratic faith. *The Eve of the Revolution* was a little book in which he tried to recapture the emotional and intellectual outlook of the American leaders as they lived through the years from 1763 to 1776. It is significant for its last paragraph which is a ringing affirmation of the values of the Declaration of Independence: "It is to these principles — for a generation somewhat obscured, it must be confessed, by the Shining Sword and the Almighty Dollar, by the lengthening shadow of Imperialism and the soporific haze of Historic Rights and the Survival of the Fittest — it is to these principles, these 'glittering generalities,' that the minds of men are turning again in this day of desolation as a refuge from the cult of efficiency and from faith in 'that which is just by experience.' " [13]

In 1920 *Our Great Experiment in Democracy* elaborated the theme of his earlier essay on the Monroe Doctrine. It is a strange book which reads as if half had been inspired by Frederick Jackson Turner and half by Charles A. Beard without any real effort to achieve a synthesis. The first part is a frank celebration of the Turner frontier thesis. Here in America, Becker wrote, our European ancestors "found freedom from tradition, and from the legal and conventional restraints of civilized society. In America they found no pope and no king, no noble lords levying toll upon the land, no Church exacting fees from the poor as the price of salvation. In America men found all the freedom of Nature." [14] Free land, Becker continued, was the most important historical factor in determining the course of American history and shaping the national character. Without it, "The United States never could have turned its back on the Old World, and its ideas and its ideals would have been borrowed from London and Paris." But the free land is gone, he wrote, and we are watching the growth of economic class divisions with wealth more and more concentrated in a few hands. As we build a new industrial frontier, we must now look back to Europe for the experience to help us deal with this problem of a plutocracy and proletariat. In Europe, the doctrine of political liberty was supposed to go along with political equality. But in France and England, without the safety valve of the frontier, some men quickly acquired great wealth and the factory worker became a pawn in the hands of the industrialist. Europeans soon learned, therefore, that if equality as an ideal was to be preserved, economic liberty needed to be curtailed. And Becker found that "In the United States the trend of thought is turning at last, as it has long since turned in Europe, from the question of the production of wealth to the question of its distribution. . . . the best traditions of the United States, the real 'spirit of this government' are wholly in favor of whatever government activity may be necessary to assure that fundamental equality of opportunity which is indispensable to true liberty and the very essence of democracy." [15]

In these years, Carl Becker, like Charles Beard, had become a prophet of industrial democracy for the United States and the whole world. And, like Beard, Becker's renewed dream was also smashed. For one who had stood so close to the millennium, it was distressingly difficult to regain the stoic calm of 1915. All the bitterness of a broken heart overflowed in a letter to his friend William E. Dodd. The war to end war and make the world safe for democracy had ended with the world no better than it had been in 1914. Becker was horrified at the way in which his ideal had become a nightmare; he now described the war as "inexplicable on any ground of reason, or common sense, or decent aspiration, or even of intelligent self-interest; on the contrary, it was as a whole the most futile, the most desolating and repulsive exhibition of human power and cruelty without compensating advantage that has ever been on earth. This is the result of some thousands of years of what men like to speak of as 'political, economic, intellectual and moral Progress.' If this is progress, what in Heaven's name would retardation be! . . . This old eighteenth century view is too naive and simple. Neither good men nor bad wanted this war. . . . The conclusion I draw is that for good men and bad, ignorant and enlightened . . . reason and aspiration and emotion — what we call principles, faith, ideals — are without their knowing it at the service of complex and subtle instinctive reactions and impulses . . . most of politics and much of business has . . . for their primary object . . . the gaining of some advantage over others; and hence there is a subtle taint of unreality and accordingly of dishonesty about these enterprises that warps and falsifies the minds of their followers. And so in my present temper politics strikes me as serving chiefly to illustrate and confirm the ancient saying: 'The human heart is deceitful and desperately wicked.' " [16]

Becker had said farewell to reform; men had tried to be creative and they had failed. He was going back to Cornell to withdraw from the world of passion and failure to the world of skepticism and success. Soon he seemed to have regained the stoic pose of 1915. When he reviewed Henry Adams' *The Degradation of the Democratic Dogma*, he began calmly by taking issue with Adams' statement that most American historians subscribed to the idea of progress. Adams was pleading with the historical profession to abandon the concept of progress and to accept the scientific thesis of the necessary dissipation of energy. But most historians, Becker argued, believed in neither progress nor Adams' version of scientific law. Instead, they studied the past without asking the larger philosophical questions implied either in progress or in the running down of the energy of the universe. Becker revealed, however, that he was still very sensitive to his loss of faith in progress when he exploded in this review in a diatribe against a young historian who was so foolish as to believe in progress. "Last spring . . . I listened to a young man describing with great enthusiasm a proposed new course designed to show the onward and upward progress of democracy — up to and including May 30, 1919. While he was expounding, my eye fell upon the cover of the *Current History* for that very month, and there I read the following words: 'Seething Caldron in Europe — Revolution — Civil War — Disorders — Anarchy!' I wondered if I was expected to teach the progress of democracy onward and upward to the Seething Caldron?" [17]

It is possible to suggest the depth of Becker's despair by watching him reach back toward the verities of his youth. Becker tried to retreat to the Midwest from which he had fled in 1916. The Midwest was still committed to isolation and Becker desperately needed to share that sense of isolation from the world's problems. His essay "Europe through the Eyes of the Middle West" is a fascinating study of a troubled mind seeking escape. In 1914, he wrote, I was living in Lawrence, Kansas, and we felt no great shock at the news of the war because Europe was a meaningless abstraction. With deceptive ease, Becker had submerged his individuality in the people; the "I" had become "we." But soon, he continued, we learned from the people in the East that Germany was the aggressor and that the United States should join the Allies against Germany. We voted for Wilson in 1916, however, trusting him to keep the peace. When war did come, we were sure that Wilson had exhausted the possibilities of preserving peace. With the war a fact, the people of Kansas decided this must become the last war fought to save Europeans from themselves. Such a view made them susceptible to the war propaganda that this was to be the war to end war, to make the world safe for democracy. They didn't really believe it but they wanted to believe it. Now the war is over and outsiders ask what we think of the treaty. And Becker answered: "Frankly, we don't think of it. The war is over, and all our purposes achieved. The Kaiser is down and out, German militarism is crushed, the Treaty of Versailles provides for the Allies . . . adequate guarantees against future aggression, and the League of Nations is set up to inaugurate a new international order. . . .

It makes us uncomfortable to think about Europe, which we understand less than we did before the war. Besides, we do not like to think." [18]

Becker, like the Kansans, desperately embraced "normalcy" in domestic and international affairs. His particular "normalcy" was to be the study of the past in terms of itself. He would be the neutral observer. But as Carl Becker had written and rewritten: Who in all eternity had discovered the historian who was merely the neutral observer? To what extent could Becker coldly and dispassionately analyze his chosen area of research, the age of the American and French revolutions? Some of his fellow historians, in reviewing his next book, *The Declaration of Independence*, felt that he had succeeded too well. But there is significant evidence that Becker had not yet discovered the formula which might harden his heart against the spiritual and intellectual home he had found in the Enlightenment during his student years at Columbia.

In the first chapter, Becker insisted that the only way to understand the Declaration was to ask what it was designed to accomplish. Its major purpose, he wrote, was to furnish a moral and legal justification for the Revolution. It accomplished this task by assuming the validity of a philosophy of natural rights which insisted that governments are instituted to preserve the rights of individuals and, therefore, derive their power from the consent of the governed. From this first premise, the Declaration then pointed to the English king who was destroying the rights of the American individuals; rebellion against his authority was necessary.

In the next chapters, Becker developed these two points. In his discussion of natural rights, he stressed that all civilized men of the eighteenth century, whether in England, France, or America, believed in their reality. Central to this eighteenth-century view was a concept of nature as the necessary location of God's law. Returning to the emphasis of his early writings, Becker stressed the great faith of the Enlightenment, a faith in nature. But in 1922 there is a hostile note in Becker's description of this secular religion that was not there in 1914: "The eighteenth century did not abandon the old effort to share in the mind of God; it only went about it with greater confidence, and had at last the presumption to think that the infinite mind of God and the finite mind of man were one and the same thing." [19]

In tracing what he called the deification of nature and the denaturing of God, Becker focused on the crucial role played by the ideas of Newton and Locke as they were popularized in the eighteenth century. He stressed that men did not read Newton and Locke but used their general reputations to support what they already believed, "that in the world of human relations as well as in the physical world, it was possible for men to 'correspond with the general harmony of nature!' "

When Becker described the way in which this philosophy was incorporated into the Declaration by Thomas Jefferson, he related the essence of the natural rights philosophy to Jefferson's literary style. Jefferson was expressing a philosophy of simplicity with a wonderful lucidity. But the style, like the philosophy, had a perfection which divorced it from life. The tough-minded Carl Becker caustically wrote: "Felicity of expression — certainly Jefferson had that; but one wonders whether he did not perhaps have too much of it. This sustained felicity gives one at times a certain feeling of insecurity, as of resting one's weight on something fragile. Jefferson's placidity, the complacent optimism of his sentiments and ideas, carry him at times perilously near the fatuous. One would like more evidence that the iron had some time or other entered his soul, more evidence of his having profoundly reflected upon the enigma of existence, of having more deeply felt its tragic import." [20]

Carl Becker knew the tragic import of existence; his personal tragedy was the failure of the Jeffersonian dream: "Founded upon a superficial knowledge of history it was, certainly; and upon a naive faith in the instinctive virtues of human kind. Yet it was a humane and engaging faith. . . . It taught that beneath all local and temporary diversity, beneath the superficial traits and talents that distinguish men and nations, all men are equal in the possession of a common humanity. . . . This faith could not survive the harsh realities of the modern world. Nationalism and industrialism . . . a more trenchant scientific criticism steadily dissolving its own 'universal and eternal law' into a multiplicity of incomplete and temporary hypotheses — these provided an atmosphere in which faith in Humanity could only gasp for breath." [21]

The anguish and frustration which tormented Becker during the early 1920's broke into the open by 1926. As Becker's heart could not abandon liberalism, so his mind could not easily pretend to a theory of historical neutrality. It was with dramatic suddenness and intensity then that Becker revealed the continued vitality of his progressive convictions in two poignant essays.

One was a paper — "What Are Historical Facts?" — delivered to the American Historical Association which revived his position of 1910. Historians, he wrote, believe that their "business is to discover and set forth the 'facts' of history." But, Becker asked of his colleagues, what is a historical fact? Any fact that is meaningful to men is meaningful because it relates to other facts. Any usable fact is a symbol "which is a generalization of a thousand and one simpler facts . . . and this generalization itself we cannot use apart from the wider facts and generalizations which it symbolizes." [22] Specific symbols, he continued, become meaningful to historians as their culture moves through time and faces new problems. Every society has a vision of its past, its present, its future, and the crucial task of the professional historian is to clarify his society's theory of the past upon which it bases its decisions about the future. But the historian has failed to accept this responsibility to enlighten his society, to make it more rational. Historical study flourished through the nineteenth century but the fruits of its research were not given to the people. As a result, mankind went into World War I without an accurate understanding of the past and of the future. Has historical research, Becker cried out, "done anything to restrain the foolishness of politicians or to enhance the wisdom of statesmen? Has it done anything to enlighten the mass of the people, or to enable them to act with greater wisdom or in response to a more reasoned purpose? Very little surely, if anything. Certainly a hundred years of expert historical research did nothing to prevent the World War, the most futile exhibition of unreason . . . ever made by civilized society." [23] Governments and peoples, he recounted, rushed into this war with undiminished stupidity, with unabated fanaticism, with an unimpaired capacity for deceiving themselves and others.

Becker now revealed the desperate nature of the inner debate that he was engaged in with the ghost of Henry Adams. From 1920 to 1940, Becker was to write often of Henry Adams and the Adams family. Almost always he dismissed the pessimism of Henry Adams as philosophically unsound. Clearly, Adams' vision of an onrushing scientific juggernaut, multiplying its power until it overwhelmed mankind, haunted Becker. And, in 1926, he called on historians to keep Adams' prophecy from becoming fact. World War I was so horrible, he declared, because of science, the cold, neutral, efficient facts of science, which allowed men to destroy themselves on an unprecedented scale. Humanity, during the nineteenth century, dedicated itself to the inhuman knowledge of science and refused to consider the human knowledge of history.

This kind of stirring enthusiasm is repeated in Becker's essay review of H. G. Wells's epic history of civilization. Wells, Becker wrote, is clearly in the tradition of the "new history" of James Harvey Robinson. And it is not surprising that this kind of history, popular before World War I, should reappear. It is natural to mankind because men must build a vision of the future and find its foundations in the past. "So long as hope springs in the human breast the 'new history' will be a recurring phenomenon." Becker related the "new history" to the great age of reform in the eighteenth century. The "new history" of Wells, like the "new history" of James Harvey Robinson in 1900, Becker declared, was a renewal of the optimistic use of history as a tool of social reform which had characterized the Enlightenment. It had become unpopular during the nineteenth century, Becker explained, because men had become pessimistic and conservative and had sought refuge from social responsibility behind the myth of scientific history. Now, however, twentieth-century man had regained faith in the possibility of progress and historians like Robinson and Wells were demonstrating the use of historical study as a guideline to that progress.

By the standards of scientific history, Wells had not written a successful book but Becker added: "A contribution to knowledge the book does not of course pretend to be; but a contribution to the meaning which we may, and indeed ought, to attach to the knowledge we have, it does very particularly pretend to be." [24] Like the *philosophes*, Wells went to the past to find a definition of values, of progress. And like the men of the Enlightenment, he defined progress as the increasing use of intelligence. Becker, who since 1919 had been unable to relate himself actively to reform movements, applauded Wells for being a reformer first and a historian second: Wells "is too much aware of being himself a part of the cosmic process, is too intent upon shaping and improving that process, is too much in the game, to be willing to stand, aloofly wrapped in the blanket of intellectual curiosity, on the side lines, with no other purpose than to observe the intricacies of the play as it goes by." [25]

The attraction of this man of great faith for the doubting Becker is painfully revealed in Becker's explanation of the source of Wells's values. "No, it is not the study of history, but present experience, which torments the soul and makes us all wish passionately to end war and suffering, that enables Mr. Wells to see the Promised Land. The Promised Land must be ahead, because — otherwise it would be too horrible!" [26]

One can guess that Becker's renewal of enthusiasm for his 1910–1914 position was not caused by mounting optimism but by deepening pessimism. In both of these essays, he had pictured a future dominated by the monstrous growth of scientific power fated to destroy humanity. This fate was inevitable as long as Becker and his contemporaries continued their stance of studied objectivity and withdrawal. But, in 1927, what was the alternative? What hope existed for a regeneration of the world or even America? The national policy was drift, world policy was drift. What could a single man, now middle-aged and soon to become old, do to arrest this horrible drift to destruction? Becker's vision of the future became unbearable and he mustered his intellectual forces to reach a new definition of history that was not so overwhelmingly tragic. His greatest book, *The Heavenly City of the Eighteenth Century Philosophers,* symbolizes his effort to escape from participation in a society whose only destiny was destruction.

Becker had reached maturity defining America as the physical embodiment of the ideals of the Enlightenment. Like Bancroft, Turner, and Beard, he had seen the fundamental frontier experience as the fulfillment of the Puritan withdrawal from medieval civilization. Until 1914, Becker had postulated history as the record of progress from the smothering complexity of Rome to the liberating simplicity of the Kansas prairie. Then with terrifying suddenness, Becker discovered that a new kind of complexity was present in the world; that, indeed, the growth of science and technology meant that this complexity must inevitably increase. History was no longer a frontier experience in which humanity moved from complexity to simplicity. History loomed as the tragic vision of Henry Adams, the destruction of humanity by its servant, science.

Now Becker rewrote his view of history from 1500 to the present to prove that the frontier thesis was still the true definition of historical trends but with one important qualification. The frontier thesis could be saved only by surrendering its traditional values. One could write that history from 1500 to the present was the history of the liberation of the mind, but of the mind only. Progress was no longer the history of the growing freedom for the whole man, the man of faith, of values, of love, of commitment. Nevertheless, Becker managed to rewrite history so that he was able to escape from the prophecy of Henry Adams; ironically, he also had to abandon his own intellectual past.

His basic strategy in this rearrangement of history was to disassociate himself from the Enlightenment. The frontier thesis had postulated that man was to escape from the entangling web of history to the firm foundation of nature. The frontier thesis had postulated that the ideal of nature had been achieved in the Enlightenment; men had escaped from the ephemeral traditions of the Middle Ages to live with the certainty of natural law. Not so, Becker now wrote: the Enlightenment is merely an extension of medieval historical tradition.

Becker began this book with a discussion of the concept of "climate of opinion," using the Middle Ages as an example of what is implied in this term. The essentials of a climate of opinion, he related, are "instinctively-held preconceptions," which control the individual's use of intelligence and logic. The preconceptions of medieval man were that "Existence was . . . a cosmic drama, composed by the master dramatist according to a central theme and on a rational plan. Finished in idea before it was enacted in fact, before the world began written down to the last syllable of recorded time, the drama was unalterable either for good or evil." Such beliefs directed men to bring logic and intelligence "to demonstrate the truth of revealed knowledge, to reconcile diverse and pragmatic experience with the rational pattern of the world as given in faith." [27] The Middle Ages was an era of both faith and reason, in which reason was employed to support faith, and this is, he wrote, the direct antithesis of the climate of opinion of twentieth-century America.

Becker, who for thirty years had related twentieth-century America with the Enlightenment, now tried to break all intellectual ties with the historical source of his values. Now he described himself and his America in terms of that nineteenth-century scientific conservatism which for half a lifetime he had so bitterly criticized. We cannot believe in faith or reason, he wrote, because, under the influence of modern science, we, of this modern century, believe only in specific facts. "We start with the irreducible brute fact, and we must take it as we find it, since it is no longer permitted to coax or cajole it, hoping to fit it into some or other category of thought on the assumption that the pattern of the world is a logical one." [28] The accumulating facts of scientific research pointed overwhelmingly to a world without pattern or logic, to a universe of constant flux in which there are no absolutes.

This willingness to live by fact rather than opinion, he continued, cuts the modern man off from the men of the Enlightenment who were men of faith and reason like their medieval ancestors. On the surface, he recounted, the *philosophes* seemed to have rejected the faith and reason of the Middle Ages and turned to the empiricism of science. But the writers of the eighteenth century used science only as a negative weapon to destroy the position of the Church and aristocracy. After claiming that no values could be accepted which did not pass the test of empirical verification, and after rejecting the principles of the *ancien regime* for failing that test, the *philosophes*, Becker found, then had faith that there was a rational order of nature which was to serve as the basis of a new and more moral civilization. Furthermore, Becker argued, the spokesmen of the Enlightenment were unable to demonstrate by their supposed commitment to scientific empiricism the existence of such a natural moral order. All they had done, he claimed, was to secularize the faith of the Middle Ages. They believed that the Heavenly City of the thirteenth century was to find earthly expression in the eighteenth century. Like the medieval theologian, the *philosophe* operated from faith and reason and not from the brute facts of existence. The *philosophe* had damned the theologian as one who dwelt in the realm of superstition and unfounded opinion. The *philosophe* argued that progress was escape from ephemeral, historical opinion to the unchanging, eternal verities of nature. But Becker defined this attempt as an utter failure because the men of the Enlightenment had tried to invest the facts of nature, the neutral facts of the empirical method, with values that sprang from opinion, from the uncertain and unscientific depths of the human heart, from history.

If then, Becker argued, we are to fulfill the Enlightenment's definition of progress as the escape from the shifting sands of historical opinion to the immutable rock of scientific fact, we must reject the values of the Enlightenment, we must renounce the ideal of a Heavenly City on earth. We must elaborate a stoic code of acceptance of the only reality, the meaningless data of science. Here in the twentieth century, he declared, we have replaced theology with the science of history which accepts things not on faith but by empirical verification. We have replaced philosophy with science and again have replaced speculation with fact. This, he affirmed, is progress, this "trend of modern thought away from an overdone rationalization of the facts to a more careful and disinterested examination of the facts themselves."

The moral lesson for Becker was clear: the men of the Enlightenment had failed to live up to their own standard of progress. They remained in the complexity of historical opinion; they had not really moved to the simplicity of scientific truth. It was only in the twentieth century that men had escaped from climates of opinion to the truth of empirically verified facts.

And if this acceptance of the empiricism of science was indeed the modern outlook, Becker could argue that Henry Adams' prophecy of the inevitable doom of society was wrong. In the first place, Becker had demonstrated that science had led men out of the complex superstitions of the medieval world to the scientific simplicity of the present. And this was simplicity because science presented men with only one fact at a time. The true scientific method disallowed Henry Adams' kind of philosophic speculation which depended on the existence of complex patterns of facts operating over time. One had to believe in faith and reason to find such patterns and the sophisticated twentieth-century man was, therefore, freed from the hobgoblins of Adams' superstitious and essentially medieval mind.

Becker had tried to find surcease from the terrors of a history which no longer offered automatic redemption to Americans by charting a complete retreat to the mindless conservatism of that nineteenth-century scientific history which he so abhorred. He failed and he was aware of his failure.

In the last chapter of *The Heavenly City* he was to admit that the twentieth-century man had not escaped from history; indeed, he would affirm that mankind lived by values and not scientific facts. This division of Becker's argument in the book marks the beginning of his final intellectual pilgrimage. The discovery that the Enlightenment was rooted in the traditions of the past was to open up a new line of thinking for Carl Becker, the child of the Enlightenment. Momentarily, he had renounced his intellectual debt to the eighteenth century which he had connected to history. But if, in the future, he were once again to admit his relationship to the *philosophes*, might he not also admit his relationship to all that rich historical tradition which he had found was the intellectual matrix of the Enlightenment? And could Carl Becker then remain a spokesman for the Jeffersonian covenant?

6 VERNON LOUIS PARRINGTON: THE COVENANT AND THE JEFFERSONIAN JEREMIAD

I N 1927 appeared the single most important book written by a historian of the frontier tradition, Vernon Louis Parrington's *Main Currents in American Thought*. It stands as the most impressive monument to the views of Turner, Beard, and Becker because it brings together within one cover all the complex and contradictory historical theories of these men. Even more, written during the 1920's, it contains all the demoralizing questions which had occurred to Turner as he watched the physical frontier disappear and which had confronted Beard and Becker as they saw their concept of an industrial frontier shattered by World War I. But, finally, the greatness of the book as a concluding testament to a dying tradition rests on the manner in which it clarifies the roots of this tradition in the eighteenth-century Enlightenment and ultimately in seventeenth-century Puritanism. Parrington's book is truly a summary of the main currents of American thought and the fatal impasse these currents had reached by the 1920's.

There is fitting drama in the appearance of this book. Born in 1871, in Aurora, Illinois, Parrington had written nothing of significance during the first decades of the twentieth century when book after book was flowing from the pens of Beard and Becker. Still more surprising, he was not even a professional historian but a teacher of English at the University of Washington.

One wonders whether the background of the book does not provide a symbolic setting for understanding the tremendous intellectual stir which Parrington created. Seen from the viewpoint of the historical profession,

98

Parrington, the unknown outsider whose life was almost over, was a voice crying from the wilderness. And this is the fundamental significance of Parrington: his was a voice crying out to his people to return to the ways of their ancestors, to reform, to purify themselves before it was too late. *Main Currents* must be seen as a great expression of that peculiar Puritan theological literary form, the Jeremiad. As the Puritan preachers had warned their people at the end of the seventeenth century that they were straying from their special relationship to God as a chosen people and must face disaster if they did not turn back from corruption to live by the national covenant, so Parrington, in the 1920's, warned his people that they must experience the terrors of history unless they too returned to the national covenant expressed by Thomas Jefferson — a covenant which promised the faithful that they might live in harmony as long as they followed nature's principles. But his was a despairing voice from the wilderness because Parrington was not able to offer any hope that the covenant could be fulfilled in urban-industrial America.

There is obvious irony in relating Parrington to New England Puritanism. The first section of his book is notorious as a scathing denunciation of the Winthrops and the Mathers. But the irony disappears when one recognizes that Parrington is criticizing the leaders of seventeenth-century New England for a failure to live by what he considered the true principles of Puritanism.

Puritanism in the sixteenth century was a revolutionary philosophy, Parrington wrote, designed to free the individual from the corporate feudal order of the medieval world. But "The far-reaching liberalisms implicit in the rejection of a hierarchical organization of the church were to discover no allies in the major premises of the system of theology accepted generally by the English Puritans." [1] These men rejected Luther to follow Calvin. And Calvin, for Parrington, represented no break from the tyrannical traditions of the Middle Ages. Indeed, Calvinism in many ways was worse than medieval culture because it looked back into the Oriental past for theological guidance.

The "Hebraized Englishmen" who founded New England, therefore, had no commitment to liberty and equality; instead they believed in a coercive hierarchy, guided by themselves, God's stewards. Among the English settlers, however, there were some like the Pilgrims and Roger Williams who represented the Lutheran rather than the Calvinist tradition of the Reformation. Parrington called these men idealists. His idealist is one who can transcend in his imagination the highly institutionalized and traditional society of the present to prophesy a new society where every man freely guides his destiny on principles that he finds in his heart.

There are times when Parrington identifies this idealist as a realist because his vision coincides with the reality of a natural society uncorrupted by the historical past. Like Becker, Beard, Turner, and Bancroft, Parrington found no ultimate reality in the changing patterns of historical society. True reality was found only in nature's principles. In seventeenth-century America, therefore, the isolated idealist, like Roger Williams, was the voice of a real future; his vision had the potential to become reality.

Free land, Parrington wrote, made possible from the very beginning of New England the formation of a new kind of man, uniquely American, the yeoman farmer. These men constituted a body of democratic freeholders who naturally believed in liberty and equality. In America, the ideal was to become real because here history ended and nature began. Unlike the common man who experienced a rebirth, however, the Puritan magistrates clung to history. "Bred up in a half-feudal world, the leaders of the Migration remained patriarchal in their social philosophy, unable to adapt old prejudices to new conditions." [2] And there is an increasing harshness in Parrington's criticism as he moves through the seventeenth century with the Puritan community. The magistrates of the first generation, like John Winthrop, he can excuse for their undemocratic behavior. They were merely acting like the semifeudal English gentlemen that they were. But the first theologians had consciously chosen Calvin rather than Luther. They were responsible for developing hierarchical theory in a land which beckoned men to freedom and equality. Parrington's anger was magnified by the theologians of the second generation who closed their minds and hearts more callously than their fathers to the frontier's call to freedom. When he came to the third generation of theologians, to a Cotton Mather who stubbornly remained a Calvinist in the midst of natural freedom, Parrington's tolerance was at an end: "The heroic qualities of an earlier age had atrophied in an atmosphere of formalism, and Boston Calvinism of the year 1690 had become a grotesque caricature of a system that in its vigor had defied the power of Rome." Look, he asked, at Cotton Mather: "Intensely emotional, high-strung and nervous, he was oversexed and overwrought. . . . What a crooked and diseased mind lay back of those eyes that were forever spying out occasions to magnify self! He grovels in proud self-abasement. He distorts the most obvious reality." [3]

New England's intellectual history during the seventeenth century, for Parrington, was full of sound and fury signifying nothing. The world of Calvinist tradition and English institutions was not the reality of New England; that reality was to be found in the yeomen, Americans who lived with nature and not with history. But he was able to close the section dealing with seventeenth-century New England on a happy note. Puritanism was dead. The eighteenth-century mind expressed the principles of nature. A first American example was the New England preacher John Wise, whose only theology was the rights of the people. Unlike Cotton Mather, Wise "understood the plain people whom he served, and he sympathized heartily with the democratic ideals then taking form in the New England villages." [4]

Parrington began the section dealing with the new century by dramatizing the importance of the frontier in the making of a truly American mind during the years between 1720 and 1776. When Parrington wrote that "A new psychology was being created by the wide spaces," he was laying the foundation for an affirmation that American thought owed nothing to European tradition. American ideals of freedom and equality were parallel to those of European liberals. But Americans came to these ideals from their experience with their free society, not by borrowing from European thinkers. Parrington stressed the term psychology when he described the growth of a native American mind. American ideals sprang from the direct personal experience of the American individual. The American Enlightenment did not come from seventeenth-century Puritanism. It did not come from the influence of the European Enlightenment. The American Enlightenment was the product of a unique way of life that had appeared because of nature's impact.

He dramatized this disjunction by contrasting Jonathan Edwards and Benjamin Franklin. Edwards he described as a tragic figure who had the intellectual potential to become a great philosopher but who wasted his talents trying to reinvigorate the decadent ideal of Puritan theology. Benjamin Franklin, on the other hand, was the first great representative of the American mind. Significantly, Parrington did not stress Franklin's role as a creative, theoretical physicist; rather Franklin was presented as a practical humanitarian, best understood as the fulfillment of Daniel Defoe's ideal — "Robinson Crusoe, the practically efficient man making himself master of his environment . . . Franklin was the visible, new-world embodiment of that dream." [5] Travel in Europe taught him the abstract economic and political theory which fitted instincts developed in his American experience. Franklin, Parrington wrote, "went abroad democratic by temperament and environment. He came back one by conviction."

In describing the impotence of Edwards' Puritan theology and the surging strength of Franklin's pragmatic humanitarianism, Parrington had quickly reached the climax of American intellectual development. The American environment, the frontier, had defeated Old World theology. The representative American thinker, Franklin of 1750, owed nothing to Europe. American thought was in harmony with American nature. But there still remained the problem of liberating the American people from symbolic bondage to the past. Parrington, in the 1920's, was in the tradition begun by Bancroft in the 1830's. Parrington, however, had to face the existence of a complex America which had developed during the nineteenth century. Unlike Bancroft, Parrington knew that Andrew Jackson had not permanently restored the simplicity of Jefferson's Arcadia. Parrington could not share Bancroft's belief that the American Revolution marked the end of history. He must find in the 1780's the sources of the complexity that had marked American history during the nineteenth century. Parrington's introduction to the place of the Revolution in American thought is a curious combination of triumph and defeat, exaltation and despair.

The Revolution, he explained, was the result of the clash between the new English policy of tightening imperial control over the colonies and the American psychology of freedom that the frontier had produced by 1763: "A popular will to self-rule had long been developing in America, and when the outbreak of hostilities clarified its latent objective, it speedily asserted a conscious republican purpose. . . . An American mind had been created by the silent pressure of environment." [6]

Like Bancroft, Parrington described the existence of a merchant aristocracy in the northern colonies and a planting aristocracy in those of the South, aristocracies which controlled the colonial assemblies and began the quarrel with the British policy. Like Bancroft, he refused to define the ultimate meaning of the Revolution in terms of the leadership of these groups. They were not shaped by American nature. They lived with history, the traditions and institutions of the European past. And so he insisted that when the crisis moved in the direction of revolution and independence, leadership passed from the cautious gentlemen like John Dickinson, who feared that revolution against England would threaten their monopoly of power, to the radical democrats like Sam Adams, who wanted a revolution to end British rule and also to end the control of the colonial aristocracies. "In the end," Parrington wrote, "the fortunes of the revolutionary movement rested with the yeomanry, and this yeomanry with its agrarian outlook and republican sympathies, was in a mood to respond to radical appeal." [7]

When the crisis culminated in the Declaration of Independence, this document reflected the outlook of the yeomen. Commentators have found that the Declaration was based on the philosophy of John Locke, Parrington wrote, but they were wrong. The Declaration of Independence "was an eloquent confirmation of native experience, a sober justification of the psychology of individualism." And, he added, this experience of freedom began early in the seventeenth century while Locke did not write until the end of this century. "The political compact had taken form in American political thought, a generation before Locke gave currency to the theory, and Jefferson was expressing native conclusions drawn from American experience . . . he made use of old-world philosophy to express and justify certain native tendencies then seeking adequate statement." [8]

The people, brought into existence by nature, had made a revolution justified by nature. The American people were free from European traditions and institutions. But, reluctantly, Parrington now had to modify the tradition of Bancroft and follow the interpretation of Charles Beard. When he first established the pattern of Puritan New England, he had mentioned that in addition to the European tradition of Calvinist theology opposed by the American fact of a free yeomanry, there was another intellectual position: that of the middle class. Parrington failed to trace this tradition past 1700 as he chose to emphasize the triumph of the yeoman children of nature over the priestly theocrats of New England. Now, however, he was forced to confess that when the Revolution was over, there was still alive in America a strong European tradition. The feudal past was banished by the Declaration of Independence; and those in America who were loyal to it, like Thomas Hutchinson and Jonathan Boucher and thousands of others, were also banished. But the middle-class merchant aristocracy had survived the war. And these were men who were not content to live in harmony with American nature; they must strive to destroy and distort nature through the profit motive they had brought from Europe. Still worse, they would use the European institution of the coercive state to achieve their goal.

With a sad resignation, Parrington had to rob the Revolution of its fruits symbolized by the doctrines of liberty and equality of the Declaration of Independence and the Articles of Confederation. The middle class began a counterrevolution when it demanded the building of a new coercive state to make possible its economic expansion. The middle class demanded that the Constitution replace the Declaration of Independence. "This marked the turning point in American development; the checking of the long movement of decentralization and the beginning of a counter movement of centralization — the most revolutionary change in three hundred years of American experience. The history of the rise of the coercive state in America, with the ultimate arrest of all centrifugal tendencies, was implicit in that momentous counter movement." [9]

As Parrington echoed Beard's thesis that a conspiracy of an alien, un-American elite had reintroduced the evil of European traditions, institutions, and power into the American Garden, he revealed a sense of moral outrage and theological despair far greater than had appeared as yet in Beard's writings. Even in the 1920's, Beard continued to have faith that industrialism would restore the Jeffersonian covenant; Parrington had no such faith. For him, 1776 symbolized the moment when heaven on earth was achieved and 1789 symbolized the moment when the natural covenant with God was broken. For Parrington, this was the awful meaning of the triumph of the Federalists. They had tricked the people into accepting complexity and thus had destroyed the possibility of an earthly peaceable kingdom; they had delivered Americans back into the terror of time.

This is the cosmic melodrama evoked by Parrington as he describes the serpent, Alexander Hamilton, who directed the Federalist conspiracy. This alien had glided into the national Garden with his foul plan to tempt the people with the apple of economic progress. He was "hard, almost brutal," he was "utterly devoid of sentiment and without a shred of idealism," he had "intellectual arrogance" and "cynical contempt" for the people.

The depth of Parrington's horror at Hamilton's success in winning the people away from their commitment to the purity and simplicity of nature and his success in bringing them to accept the doctrine of English materialistic progress is demonstrated by his inability to bring his book to its logical conclusion with the establishment of the leviathan state of the Federalists in 1789. Parrington had told us that the covenant was irretrievably lost because the hearts of the people had been corrupted by the lure of

economic growth. Guided by Hamilton they began to build the foundations of industrialism which would obliterate agricultural America. And
yet, Parrington, as a high priest of the Jeffersonian covenant, refused to
surrender his personal faith. It almost seems as if he hoped that if he repeated the sacred phases of George Bancroft, a miracle might occur and
the Garden might be restored.

Even here, however, as Parrington prepared the elements of the ritual
drama in which a representative hero of the people was to emerge and lead
the real Americans in victorious battle against the serpent and his alien
and un-American host and thus restore the covenant, we are aware of the
implacable facts of history which will make this a ceremony without
meaning. For Parrington, 1800, not 1828, had to be Armageddon, because, unlike Bancroft and Turner, he could not claim that the victory of
Jackson was the fulfillment of progress in perfect primitivism. In his historical narrative, industrialism was marching forward in seven league
boots by 1828. If Hamilton and his alien doctrine of economic progress
were to be stopped, it must be done by the first great prophet of the covenant, Jefferson.

For a moment Parrington wrote religious poetry as if it were the factual historical record. The people, he began, lost political control in the
1780's because they were too naive. From their experience with nature,
they had become democrats. But they did not know how to define democracy in abstract terms. And so they were confused when the middle-class
aristocracy said to them, trust us, we are committed to your values. At
Philadelphia, behind closed doors, of course, the founding fathers had
written a document which would create a leviathan state but when they
emerged, they said to the people: We have conserved individualism and
decentralization. And the people, in their innocence, believed them. When
the French Revolution occurred, however, it clarified the abstract principles of democracy and the American people suddenly saw that they had
been cheated by false leaders. They immediately decided to express their
general will and smash this alien aristocracy and its artificial institutions.
They looked for a representative hero who would implement their will and
destroy their enemies. They found him in the person of Thomas Jefferson,
" 'the product of the first West in American history . . . Jefferson loved
his backwoods neighbors, and he, in turn, was loved by them.' " [10] Together Jefferson and the people marched on the citadel of the enemy and
took power away from Hamilton and the Federalist middle-class aristoc-

racy. In 1800, the people had regained control of their nation; they had restored the principles of 1776; they had saved the covenant: "The age of theology was gone, the age of political speculation was passing, the age of constitution building was over. Disintegration had come upon every system of caste brought from the old world; the free economics of a de-centralized society had proved a sufficient solvent to destroy the principle of monarchy and of aristocracy, and prepare the American mind for a venture in republicanism." [11]

This was the ritual drama but the miracle had not occurred. The people had not been saved from the corruption of English materialism which blackened their hearts and twisted their minds. Jefferson's political power in 1800 could not stop the growth of industrialism because the new economic system grew out of the false religion of progress to which the people had become committed. "A new romanticism of the middle class was eventually to shoulder aside the aspirations of gentleman and farmer alike, and refashion America after its own ideal." [12] The covenant could not be saved when the people were unfaithful.

Volume II of this trilogy is entitled *The Romantic Revolution in America*. Surveying the years 1800–1860, this Puritan Jeremiad revealed the horror of history which awaited the people when they abandoned the covenant. This first experience with the false romantic faith of progress would lead directly to the Civil War. But once again we learn of Parrington's continuing hope for a miracle. This was a book which also described the appearance of a good romanticism dedicated to the memory of the covenant which would challenge Hamilton's false creed for control of the people's convictions.

The structure of this second volume revolves around the conflict of self-interest that set American against American and led to the horror of a brothers' war in 1861. In the Northeast, men turned to industrialism as the way to get rich; this sectional self-interest became an economic imperialism which must dominate the nation and exploit the other regions. In the South, the expanding cotton kingdom offered the way to rapid wealth and created again a regional self-interest that became an economic imperialism which worked desperately to dominate the nation for its own ambitions. Most tragically, the expanding West, which should have been most true to Jeffersonian agrarianism, surrendered to the siren call of economic success. Parrington forced himself to write of the spread of English values into the valley of democracy: "Meanwhile in the Inland Empire was arising an economics that looked with little favor on the imperialisms of eastern capitalism or southern slavery; an economics equalitarian in temper, decentralizing in impulse; nourished on the idealism of the Declaration of Independence, but interpreting it to mean the natural right of every free citizen to satisfy his acquisitive instinct by exploiting the national resources in the measure of his shrewdness. Democratic in professions, it was middle-class in spirit and purpose." [13]

The new romanticism of the middle class with its English origins refused to admit the economic basis of politics. By obscuring the relationship of political forms to economic structure, this romanticism was able to persuade the people that they could build a complex economic structure and still retain a simple, democratic, and harmonious political life. In contrast then to the romantic realism of the natural man and the true American, Parrington described the false and ultimately vicious combinations of romanticism and realism which captured the minds of the conflicting regions.

In the South, intellectual leadership passed from cosmopolitan Virginia to provincial South Carolina. Here the great new political theorist was John C. Calhoun. At first glance, Calhoun seemed to be a defender of the Jeffersonian tradition. He recognized the danger of the Hamiltonian philosophy with its doctrine of the leviathan state in service to a plutocracy. He fought to check the growth of this un-American position and to preserve the Jeffersonian doctrines of agrarianism and local autonomy. But his romantic vision was only that of a South dominated by a slaveholding planter class. In the end, he was a realist of the same type as the Hamilton he opposed. He defended a special class interest. His romanticism led to an economic realism that was narrow and selfish.

Calhoun put Jeffersonianism in a vulnerable position to be attacked by the industrial Northeast. Calhoun "erected a last barrier against the progress of middle-class ideals — consolidation in politics and standardization in society; against a universal cash-register evaluation of life: and the barrier was blown to pieces by the guns of the Civil War." But his philosophy was "disastrous to the vital democratic principle of decentralized powers. In championing a Greek democracy, Calhoun affronted the latent idealism of America, and the harm he did to agrarian democracy was incalculable." [14]

In the tradition of Turner, Parrington saw the democratic West as the region which would thwart the evil ambitions of the slavocracy. But Parrington had to write of the terrible irony that Lincoln, a Jeffersonian, destroyed the chattel slavery of the South only inadvertently to strengthen the industrial slavery of the North.

Parrington began his description of the new West with the same enthusiasm as Turner had a generation earlier. "Taught by experience the worth of certain Jeffersonian principles, they [the pioneers] took seriously the doctrine of equality and proposed to put it into practice. . . . Springing up naturally on the frontier, the practice of democracy received from it a new validity and became the determining factor in the nationalism that America was creating in the early years of the nineteenth century. . . . Democracy became the common faith of the West, and in becoming the common faith of the West it was put in the way of becoming the common faith of America." [15]

Again Parrington had forgotten himself. Once more, he was the spokesman of a triumphant tradition unchallenged by industrial America. Here stood Bancroft's Jackson, the simple, unspoiled son of nature. No philosopher he, Parrington wrote; Jackson's "conclusions were the reactions of a simple nature of complete integrity, in contact with plain fact. . . . He remained to the last the product of an earlier domestic economy." As in the beginning with Bancroft, Parrington's Jackson rode out of the West to destroy the last vestiges of eastern aristocracy and to return the government to the people. "The driving force of the new Democracy was the same class-feeling that had done service a generation before, the will to destroy the aristocratic principle in government. This conscious class-feeling had been strengthened by the spread of the dogma of equalitarianism through the frontier." [16]

But Parrington, unlike Bancroft, had to recognize that equal in importance to Jackson on the frontiers of the new West was Henry Clay. Like Calhoun, he had abandoned the absolute principles of nature to follow the shifting, relativistic values of historical class interest: ". . . he was an opportunist who shifted from the older domestic economy to the later capitalistic, without comprehending the significance of the change. . . . Clay was a born politician who rarely came to grips with reality." [17] Taking Clay as the representative westerner, Parrington told the painful tale of the seduction of the pioneer by the capitalistic outlook which taught him that abundant land, coupled with an exploding population and easy credit, made possible quick profit from land speculation. The average westerner struggled with his Jeffersonian faith, symbolized by Jackson, and his middle-class acquisitiveness, symbolized by Clay, and for Parrington, "In such a contest the principle of Whiggery must eventually triumph. . . . Economics and psychology were daily arguing in its behalf."

While he must write that Clay's Whig party triumphed and while Clay had brought the West into alliance with Daniel Webster's industrial Northeast to oppose Calhoun's South and drive the country toward civil war, Parrington could not break completely from the Bancroft tradition and describe the Civil War as a total defeat of Jeffersonian principles. For Bancroft and Turner, the war had dignity because the free spirit of the frontier had defeated the tyrannical and foreign spirit of slavery, that great and open affront to the Declaration of Independence. To continue this tradition, Parrington contradicted the over-all theme of his book, the triumph of capitalism over Jeffersonian agrarianism, and reasserted the role of Lincoln as the savior of the Jeffersonian republic against the aggressive threat of the slavocracy. "The equalitarian West that bred Andrew Jackson bred Lincoln also, a man with the same homespun mind, the same sterling integrity of nature, the same instinctive democracy, but shaped by an environment in which the new philosophy of progress had displaced the older agrarianism. The road of middle-class ideals he traveled further than Jackson, but in the end he also turned back to pick up once more the democratic faith." [18]

Earlier, Parrington had described the Civil War as the result of the clash of economic imperialism, North against South. But now he argued that northern capitalism, led by Daniel Webster and Henry Clay, refused to face the moral evil of slavery. The men of selfish class interest were willing to compromise with this monstrous system and allow it to remain a constant stain on the honor of a nation dedicated to the democratic principle. It was Lincoln, in his "House Divided" speech, Parrington declared, who broke through the cant of the Whig leaders and placed the Republican party on the basis of moral principle rather than on expediency: ". . . he went back in a day of sordid imperialisms to the earlier liberalism of the great Virginian, seeking to rescue the idealism of the Declaration of Independence from the desecration of the market place where it was openly flouted." [19]

Parrington was trying to make Lincoln into a Jeffersonian hero who attempted to reshape the Civil War from a meaningless power struggle into an Armageddon which might restore the covenant. But the major thrust of Parrington's argument was that the war strengthened industrialism and moved the nation still further away from Jefferson's agrarian republic. If he was to salvage any hope from this hideous half century, he must find it among the New England transcendentalists who were attempting to inspire their compatriots to repel the onward march of materialism.

When Turner was faced with the disappearance of the frontier, he had been forced to try to demonstrate that democracy was a tradition which could survive the disappearance of free land. Parrington was now caught up in this logical problem. If democracy was to be saved in the twentieth century, it must be a tradition which transcended particular environments because it had such deep roots in the past that it could survive the challenge of industrialism. And so we find Parrington rehabilitating Puritanism in order to provide a democratic foundation for the New England renaissance.

Puritanism, he wrote, was dualistic; it had one theme of theological conservatism; it also had a theme of ethical concern. By 1830, this theme of ethical commitment had broken from its bondage to theological abstractions and was free at last to bring the best of New England minds to champion democracy. The forward thrust of democracy within Puritanism, Parrington declared, had brought about the Unitarian rebellion against Congregationalism by 1800. But, he added, now that the conservative traditions of Puritan theology were broken, the intrinsic democracy within Puritanism was still not free to express itself. Now it was restrained by the conservatism of the capitalistic enterprise to which most Unitarians paid homage. Daniel Webster, who had been a Jeffersonian in his youth, was identified by Parrington as the man most responsible for keeping New England from fulfilling its democratic promise. As the majority of New Englanders followed Webster toward the materialism of the Whig position, there was, however, a counter movement toward idealism led by William E. Channing which was to reach fulfillment in the transcendentalism of Ralph Waldo Emerson.

It is fascinating to follow Parrington from his commitment to the empirical rationalism of Jefferson to the transcendental idealism of Emerson. Throughout his first volume, Parrington had praised the tradition of Locke which denied innate ideas; he had praised the tradition of empiricism which denied Platonic ideals. As the frontier had disintegrated medieval society, men could use common sense to establish harmony with nature. But now the frontier was gone, a new historical society had appeared and conservatives like Webster argued from the authority of Locke that man must adjust to the new reality of that society. They argued that there were no realities beyond those of present experience. Parrington approved Emerson's rebellion against bondage to the established order in the name of a transcendent ideal. He now sympathized with idealism which affirmed the eternal validity of nature's principles above and beyond the shifting patterns of historical society. But Parrington claimed that Emerson had not committed himself to the abstract metaphysics of Europe; he had committed himself to a living faith. "Transcendentalism," he wrote, "it must always be remembered, was a faith rather than a philosophy; it was oracular rather than speculative, affirmative rather than questioning; and it went to Germany to find confirmation of its faith, not to reëxamine its foundations. Faith preceded metaphysics, and if the metaphysics had been lacking intuition would have supplied its place, poetic inspiration would have sufficed the needs of transcendental minds." [20]

Emerson, for Parrington, was a hero in his rejection of the new economic realism of Webster, a philosophy which defined man as an economic animal interested only in the acquisition of material gain. He was heroic in his rejection of the paternalism of the Whig state, of the Whig compromise on the moral issue of slavery, of Whig complacency in the face of the new economic slavery of the factory. "In all this — in the doctrine of the minimized state, of the sacred rights of the individual, of the wholesomeness of an agricultural life; in his concern for social justice and his tenderness for the poor and exploited among men — Emerson proved himself a child of the romantic eighteenth century." [21]

Parrington found even greater transcendental heroes than Emerson in the figures of Henry David Thoreau and Theodore Parker. Emerson was the great poet of transcendentalism but Thoreau and Parker put the natural principles of that poetry into practical action in a way that Emerson, the man of contemplation, did not. When Thoreau went to live at Walden, when he went to jail rather than support the Mexican War with his taxes, he made Jeffersonian principles his personal reality. Parrington eulogized the Thoreau in whom "the potent liberalisms let loose on the world by Jean Jacques, came to fullest expression in New England. He was the completest embodiment of the *laissez-faire* reaction against a regimented social order, the severest critic of the lower economics that frustrate the dreams of human freedom." [22]

In Parrington's estimation, Theodore Parker surpassed Emerson because he worked to provide rational and scientific proof for his transcendental faith. He searched through history and used anthropology to find proof that the human spirit must always break loose from historical institutions and traditions which impede the course of human progress. But he showed also how America "had thrown off theocracy, aristocracy, and monarchy," only to set in their places the "institution of money — the master of all the rest." Parker, Parrington wrote, was the last of the great Puritan preachers who cried out against the corruption of his nation.

By 1861, however, Parrington had to confess, the transcendental renaissance was in decline. The honest and realistic criticism of Emerson, Thoreau, and Parker was replaced by the unrealistic idealism of James Russell Lowell. Lowell tried to pretend that transcendental idealism could exist in a society dedicated to money-making. He wished to believe that democracy had no relation to economic structure. In this romantic attitude, Lowell became symbolically representative of middle-class America after the Civil War. He and this middle class ignored the real meaning of the Civil War. Cheering the defeat of slavery, they forgot that Jeffersonian agrarianism with its philosophy of individualism and decentralization had also been defeated. They forgot that now the nation was committed to "the path of an unquestioning and uncritical consolidation, that was to throw the coercive powers of the centralizing state into the hands of the new industrialism." [23]

If Parrington had brought America to the verge of tragedy in 1800 at the end of his first volume, he had now placed his country directly within tragedy, within the flow of history, by 1860. But as a Jeremiah, he must believe in the possibility that his nation might return to its covenant with nature. He must believe that the ideal could become real again. He must believe that man had the freedom to transcend history. And, certainly, Parrington believed that since historical society was ephemeral, it was unreal. Capitalistic values, like those of medieval society, must eventually be superseded. But in the frontier tradition, Parrington believed that it was free land which had allowed European man to step outside of the medieval tradition and to become an American, to live by natural principles. Now the American frontier was inundated by another society dedicated to the European tradition of capitalism. There was no frontier of physical nature to allow the people to escape from this society and its traditions to live by the principles of nature. Parrington, unlike Beard, did not believe that industrialism was a frontier force that could destroy capitalism. Like Becker, Parrington described industrialism as a mushrooming complexity.

How could the Jeffersonian in America after 1800 be anything but an Emersonian transcendentalist, stepping spiritually but not physically outside of his society, asking exceptional individuals to return to the covenant in the realm of the inner life but reconciled to the inability of the masses to live by the covenant? How could Parker destroy the evils of capitalism when capitalism was embedded in the reality of industrialism? How could transcendentalism survive the Civil War which so clearly marked the triumph of industrialism?

In the final and unfinished volume of his epic, *The Beginnings of Critical Realism in America,* dealing with the years 1860–1920, Parrington brought to sharp focus all the dilemmas of the frontier thesis without finding solutions for any of them. He had retreated from the empiricism of Locke to transcendental idealism in the previous volume; now he was about to try to make an even more fundamental reversal. If the democratic values created by the frontier were to be saved in an industrial society, he argued, men would have to cooperate. Liberty and equality had to be supported by fraternal cooperation. Why had Americans in 1865 failed to see this? Why did they refuse to see that there might still be time to check the evils of industrialism if they acted immediately?

Parrington's answer is surprising to those who have read his rhapsodic commitment to frontier individualism in his first two volumes: It was the frontier which had made Americans so individualistic that they were unable to cooperate. As this awful thought filled his mind, Parrington was led to ask another question. Why were Americans so easily corrupted after 1800? Why were they seduced so easily into following English capitalism and into abandoning the Jeffersonian covenant? His answer was again the antisocial individualism developed by contact with the frontier. He had reached a point of almost total irony. The frontier, which had produced the democratic man, had also led to his destruction. Bitterly he wrote, "Having swept across the continent to the Pacific coast like a visitation of locusts, the frontier spirit turned back upon its course to conquer the East, infecting the new industrialism with a crude individualism, fouling the halls of Congress, despoiling the public domain, and indulging in a huge national barbecue." [24]

If Parrington now found the frontiersman to be a cannibalistic destroyer of the virgin land which had provided Americans with the opportunity to be reborn, where could he find democratic ideals which might provide the ideological foundation for a popular uprising to restore the

Jeffersonian covenant? As Parrington had been forced to admit that the American pioneer after 1800 was incapable of being regenerated by physical nature because he had become corrupted by English capitalism, he had been forced to find a series of Old World refuges for the democratic ideal. For those Americans who were able to transcend the alien capitalist culture, there must be a democratic beacon that could inspire them to rebuild the Jeffersonian republic. Parrington, who had gloried in the provincialism of Franklin and Jefferson and who had urged the isolation of eighteenth-century America from European ideology, now had no choice but to plead with Americans to look backward to Europe, to Puritanism, to German romanticism, to French humanitarianism in order to find the democratic ideal in uncorrupted form.

This is the setting for the tragic irony in Parrington's treatment of Mark Twain, for here "at last was an authentic American — a native writer thinking his own thoughts, using his own eyes, speaking his own dialect — everything European fallen away, the last shred of feudal culture gone, local and western yet continental." [25] Here at last was a writer who was the child of the frontier — and Parrington found him a failure as a man and writer. Twain failed, for Parrington, because he had no sense of social responsibility, no sense of being a member of society, no feeling of fraternity for his fellow Americans. His only real values were material. "And when in the end the fool's gold turned to ashes in his mouth, as a frontiersman still he pursued his way alone, a solitary pioneer exploring the universe, seeking a homestead in an ironical cosmos, until overwhelmed by the intolerable solitude he made mock at all the gods. What a commentary on the Gilded Age!" [26]

The tragedy of Mark Twain, for Parrington, was that he was a provincial. He was a nationalistic frontiersman, unable to see that he no longer defined the frontier in Jeffersonian terms. He was such a prisoner of English middle-class romanticism that he could not penetrate behind the façade of alien culture which masqueraded as Americanism. And he could find no inspiration from European prophets of democracy like Rousseau.

In dramatic contrast to Twain, Parrington presented the figure of Walt Whitman. Whitman stood alone amidst the corruption of the 1870's as a beacon of democratic hope because he was strengthened by the faith of Rousseau. Alone among the writers of his time he recognized the fundamental importance of the concept of fraternity. Whitman, for Parrington, was the greatest nineteenth-century American because he searched for and rediscovered the philosophy of the Enlightenment. Whitman, unlike Twain, was a cosmopolitan, who transcended the Gilded Age to look abroad for inspiration.

In his loving description of Whitman, Parrington was forced to reveal the very heart of his own personal dilemma. Whitman, he wrote, "accepted the twin duties laid upon him: to make clear to America her present failure in the great adventure — how far she had fallen short hitherto of any adequate democratic reality; and to mark out afresh the path to the Canaan of democratic hopes — reviving the early hopes of the Enlightenment and drawing in lovelier colors the democratic Utopia dreamed of for a hundred years." [27] But Whitman at the end of the 1870's was hard pressed to give concrete outlines to his democratic prophecy. Speaking from the east coast, Whitman had projected his democratic vistas into the West but the West had failed, and Parrington wrote that Whitman more and more had to project his hopes farther and farther into the future. Whitman was forced to cry out, "I seem to be reaching for a new politics — for a new economy. I don't quite know what, but for something." Whitman criticized middle-class America for falling short of the ideals of the Enlightenment and so did Parrington. Whitman had faith that somehow, someday, America would fulfill these ideals and so did Parrington. Whitman had hoped that these ideals would be fulfilled by the American heritage of nature, the West, and so had Parrington.

Without the hope of the West, Whitman in 1870 still had faith and so did Parrington in 1920. But every year between 1870 and 1920, every year of Parrington's lifetime, industrialism became more massive, the cities more oppressive, and the West receded. The faith of the Enlightenment postulated a free individual and, for Americans, how could the individual be free without the frontier? How could the individual be free within the smothering context of an urban-industrial society which re-created in America the conditions of European history?

Parrington knew no method of freeing man from history except the method of the physical frontier. Experiencing American life during the years of the progressive movement, Parrington had believed that the ideals of the Enlightenment might triumph over America's business civilization. But, like Whitman, he was forced "to find the support for humanitarian democracy in a dying West; a West that was dying physically and in his own hopes." Before the West died, however, it rallied America to one last effort to preserve the Jeffersonian covenant. "For upwards of a half a century creative political thinking in America was largely western agrarian, and from this source came those democratic ideas that were to provide the staple of a later liberalism." [28] He affirmed that the western farmers had transcended anarchic individualism to realize that their true values were liberty, equality, and fraternity, and that a cooperative common-wealth built by social planning was necessary to retain these values. And then this agrarian vision captured the minds of eastern intellectuals who forged progressivism. But the plutocracy, aided by World War I, Parring-ton lamented, smashed the progressive movement. And when the forces of capitalism won the field in 1920, what hope was left for the Whitman dream?

Under his own definition of realism as economic determinism, Parring-ton insisted that democracy depended upon property relations, the pat-tern of the small farm, and, after 1920, industrial property was clearly triumphant. The farmers had rallied to defend Jeffersonianism and they had lost. There was no longer a substantial basis of agrarian reality upon which to establish the ideals of the Enlightenment. But Parrington still re-fused to accept defeat. The last lines of his book are an appeal to the young men of the 1920's not to abandon Jefferson's ideals. After all, he argued, industrialism was part of history and history changed. Only physical na-ture was permanent; history was ephemeral and nature was the final re-ality. The young men must keep faith in this reality and the possibility of reachieving the good society built on natural principles sometime in the future.

Parrington's last attack, therefore, was not on an industrial order that might pass but upon an outlook that led young men to accept industrial-ism as inevitable. Accompanying the development of the world of the fac-tory, he reported, was an emphasis on physical science. By the beginning of the twentieth century, physics had gained great prestige and the central doctrine of this physics was determinism. A final vision of American his-tory haunted Parrington's last years. American history had been the es-cape from the disharmony and pessimism of Europe to the harmony and optimism of Jefferson's America. But after Jefferson, disharmony had come to America and with it pessimism, the pessimism of a deterministic science that "was an unconscious return to the dark spirit long before brought hither by Puritanism from the complexities of English society — the spirit that dominated Calvinistic dogma before it disintegrated in the freedoms made possible by the great dispersion." [29]

Parrington had written three volumes which traced the rise and decline of an American imagination; he had described the escape of free men from European history to the establishment in the new world of the Jeffersonian covenant with nature; he had told of the neglect of that covenant by the people, neglect which brought them back into the toils of European history. Was it too late to turn back? Parrington would not admit that the Jeffersonian covenant had been irretrievably lost. There was still hope if the faith did not perish with Parrington's generation. As long as there were faithful, the covenant was alive. If only he could persuade the young men to give up the false values of determinism and cynicism! If only he could reinspire the young with the beauties of the ancient faith! But all he could offer was faith. In Parrington's history, there was no reasonable ground for hope that the covenant could be restored; the economic basis of Jeffersonian democracy, the freehold farm, had vanished forever.

7 BEARD: THE COVENANT THREATENED BY INSTITUTIONAL POWER

P ARRINGTON'S J EREMIAD offered no hope to the faithful because his historical analysis announced the destruction of the physical basis of the Jeffersonian covenant by the scientific, business, and industrial forces of the nineteenth century. He made the impossible request of Americans that they return to a way of life which no longer existed. If Parringtonian pessimism was to be overcome, a historian must persuade the people that the Jeffersonian absolute had withstood the perils of historical corruption during the nineteenth century and remained a living fact in the 1920's. This was to be the self-conscious role of Charles Beard until his death in 1948.

During the middle years of the 1920's, Beard began to find a new interpretation of American history that gave him hope for the future and he passionately tried to share this viewpoint with his fellow Americans. It was a vision that synthesized his previous belief in a technological frontier with the traditional frontier thesis of Bancroft and Turner. Jefferson, whom Beard had dismissed as irrelevant in 1914, was to be recognized as the patron saint of that unique American civilization taken out of history by the beneficent presence of nature.

Now Beard argued that, since the frontier had removed America from the disharmony of the feudal European past and had created here a classless democracy without a hierarchical social structure, industrialism could play a unique role in the New World. Parrington was wrong, for Beard, when he equated industrialism with the English middle-class philosophy of acquisitiveness. Industrialism was really the economy of producers who

118

shared the values of Jefferson's agricultural producers. And this industrialism was destined to destroy the parasitical businessmen who had captured the control of the country from the agrarians during the nineteenth
century. This was the great difference between the United States and Europe. Businessmen had taken control away from feudal leaders in Europe.
If industrialism destroyed business leadership there, it would merely restore the feudal past. But when industrialism destroyed business leadership
in the United States, it would restore the democratic past of Jeffersonian
yeomen.

This was the enthusiastic, hopeful gospel Beard preached in his many
essays and books during the 1920's and 1930's. But it was accompanied
by a somber warning. Industrialism would restore the American heritage
of democracy only if the nation followed a course of isolation. Dramatically, he pictured a future that was to be either a return to Eden or a de-
scent into Hell. The people must choose. Here was a true Jeremiad. The
people could follow the siren call of eastern businessmen who tempted
them with the lure of easy wealth through foreign trade. They could sell
their souls into political bondage to an imperialistic aristocracy which
would take them into countless foreign adventures, culminating in a world
war. Or they could listen to the true patriotic prophets who would lead
them back to the republican virtues of the founding fathers — simplicity,
native democracy, isolation, and eternal harmony.

The situation was all so clear, the decision so necessary, except that
Beard faced a false prophet of terrible persuasiveness, the president of the
United States, Franklin Delano Roosevelt. The agony of Beard's struggle
against this destroyer of the American Garden of Eden was all the more
terrible because he saw Roosevelt as standing close to the great Truth.
Beard was to struggle mightily with this fallen hero to restore him to a
position of righteous leadership of the Jeffersonian covenant. For Beard,
a moment with Roosevelt and the balance might be swung and Roosevelt
put on the path that would allow him to lead his people back to the Jeffersonian Arcadia. But the moment did not come and the forces of evil led
the country into the disharmony of European history.

Beard began this great cycle of historical preaching in 1927 with a massive survey of the American past, *The Rise of American Civilization*. Like
Parrington, Beard stressed the development of the yeoman farmer in the
New World. And, as he summed up the first half of the eighteenth century,
he too found the yeomen becoming more American as they pushed West:

"They were not peasants, in the European sense of the word, surrounded by agricultural resources already exploited and encircled by ruling orders of landlords and clergy armed with engines of state and church for subduing laborers to social discipline. On the contrary, these marching pioneers were confronted by land teeming with original fertility, by forests and streams alive with game and fish and they were, under the sun and stars, their own masters. In these circumstances, a new psychology was evoked, making a race of men and women utterly different in spirit from those who dwelt on the great manors of New York and Maryland, on the wide Southern plantations, and in the villages of the Old World."[1] These pioneers, said Beard, were the most American of the Americans.

There existed in the colonies, however, an un-American aristocracy, "a ruling class experienced in the art of government and commanding economic resources of great magnitude."[2] Continuing Bancroft's tradition, Beard declared that this class carried the burden of the quarrel with England for selfish economic reasons until 1775. Then as miraculously as for Bancroft in the 1830's, Beard in the 1920's found the "people" taking control of the struggle. On the eve of the Revolution, Beard stated, ". . . it seems that a very small per cent of the colonists were politically active." But with the Declaration of Independence, the "people" became dominant in "this mass movement in which preachers, pamphleteers, committees, lawyers, and state governments advanced the revolutionary cause."[3]

For Beard, the backbone of this popular uprising was the yeoman farmer. The farmers destroyed the tyrannical and complex institutions of the British Empire, ". . . pulling down the elaborate superstructure and making the local legislatures, in which the farmers had the majorities, supreme over all things. . . . the radical leaders realized their ideal in a loose association of sovereign states; in the Articles of Confederation, their grand ideals were fairly mirrored."[4]

Beard briefly repeated his thesis that this democracy was defeated by the conspiracy of the un-American aristocracy who imprisoned the people in the tyranny of institutions again by creating the Constitution which "reestablished in effect the old British system of politics, economics, and judicial control."[5] And then he pushed rapidly forward to Thomas Jefferson, who took the control of this national state away from the alien Hamilton and returned it to the people. Jefferson, Beard wrote, is our first great representative hero. Jefferson turned his back on Europe and on the Atlantic coast, so influenced by centuries of contact with Europe, and looked to the West where the true America would emerge. And Beard paid poetic homage to the West of Jefferson's vision, to the West of Bancroft and Turner:

"It was a marvelous empire of virgin country that awaited the next great wave of migration at the close of the eighteenth century. As the waters of the Tigris, the Euphrates, and the Nile had invited mankind to build its civilization along their banks . . . so the valley of the Mississippi now summoned the peoples of the earth to make a new experiment in social economy in the full light of modern times. . . .

"The rolling tide of migration that swept across the mountains and down the valleys, spreading out through the forests and over the prairies, advanced in successive waves. In the vanguard was the man with the rifle — grim, silent, and fearless. He loved the pathless forest, dense and solitary, carpeted by the fallen leaves of a thousand years and fretted by the sunlight that poured through the Gothic arches of the trees. . . . and where the campfire at night flared up into the darkness of knitted boughs as the flaming candles on the altar of a cathedral cast their rays high into the traceries of the vaulted roof. . . .

"In this immense domain sprang up a social order without marked class or caste, a society of people substantially equal in worldly goods, deriving their livelihood from one prime source — labor with their own hands on the soil. . . .

"In its folkways and mores there was a rugged freedom — the freedom of hardy men and women, taut of muscle and bronzed by sun and rain and wind, working with their hands in abundant materials, shaping oak from their own forests and flax from their own fields to the plain uses of a plain life, content with little and rejoicing in it, rearing in unaffected naturalness many children to face also a career of hard labor offering no goal in great riches or happiness in a multitude of things. . . . all satisfied by the unadorned epic of Christianity inherited from their fathers." [6]

Like Parrington, Beard had indulged in nostalgia in writing about the early nineteenth-century frontier. Now he had to chart the corruption of this Eden by the selfish materialism of European middle-class values which submerged democracy under the vulgarity of emerging plutocracy. Temporarily, the un-Americans might introduce disharmony but Beard could still promise the re-establishment of harmony. And the greatest example of disharmony in nineteenth-century America Beard also explained in terms that paralleled those of Parrington. The dynamic industrialism of the Northeast collided with the dynamic imperialism of the southern planter and since the destiny of the country was to be industrialism, the plantation economy was fated to be destroyed: ". . . the armed conflict had been only one phase of the cataclysm, a transitory phase . . . ending in the unquestioned establishment of a new power. . . . While the planting class was being trampled in the dust — stripped of its wealth and political power — the capitalist class was marching onward in seven league boots." [7]

Like Parrington, Beard pictured the Gilded Age as an orgy of money-making without manners or morals. Unlike Parrington, however, Beard did not associate this age of corruption with the people. Instead he argued that the philosophy of grab was limited to a small plutocracy which achieved such great financial power that Beard likened them to the leaders of the Roman Empire. In 1890 the financial aristocracy in the new Rome, New York, seemed invulnerable: "Roads from four continents now ran to the new Appian way — Wall Street — and the pro-consuls of distant provinces paid homage to a new sovereign. The land of Washington, Franklin, Jefferson, and John Adams had become a land of millionaires and the supreme direction of its economy had passed from the owners of farms and isolated plants and banks to a few men and institutions near the center of its life." [8]

But Beard immediately found evidence of a revolt of the people against this un-American rule. The farmers were in rebellion; labor was in rebellion; and the middle class was beginning to rebel. Here was the great difference that separated Beard's reading of nineteenth-century history from that of Parrington and which gave him grounds for hope. Beard distinguished between the plutocracy and the American middle class. The American plutocracy had tried to entrench its power by bringing in European immigrants who were content with the entertainment provided by their masters: "Vaudeville shows, prize fights, circuses, dime museums, and cheap theaters, like the spectacles of ancient Rome, kept countless millions happy in penury." And Beard added, the American plutocracy chose Catholic workers because they knew that the Catholic Church would encourage their political passivity. "The Catholic Church, with its gorgeous ceremonials and its sublime consolations for suffering and wretchedness, followed the poor everywhere." Beard's dramatic rhetoric now expressed the wrath of the Puritan prophet denouncing those who had defiled the Jeffersonian temple: "Not since the patricians and capitalists of Rome scoured the known world for slaves . . . had the world witnessed such a deliberate overturn of a social order by masters of ceremonies." [9]

Beard knew, however, that the people would successfully resist these efforts to destroy the real America. The people would fight back and restore republican purity and simplicity: "Between the urban masses with their circuses and prize-fights and the plutocracy with its 'palatial' mansions and its social aspirations stretched a wide and active middle class engaged in professional, mercantile, and clerical pursuits. It was within this group that the early Puritan characteristics of thrift, sobriety, and self-denial appeared to survive and unfold in the most natural fashion." [10]

The people were able to attack the plutocracy without going to Europe to borrow from socialistic doctrines which were just as materialistic as those of the plutocracy. Instead the Puritan middle class developed its own alternative to acquisitive capitalism in the religious philosophy of the Social Gospel. No great social philosophers appeared in America to speak for reform, Beard recounted, because the reform movement was the effort of the people to restore the commonsense Christian ethics which had marked the Jeffersonian republic in 1800. And now the people made a successful reformation in destroying the power of the plutocracy with its protective ideology of English capitalism: ". . . by a gradual and peaceful operation was effected a transfer of economic goods greater in value than the rights shifted from the French nobility to the peasants by the national assembly. . . . historians now recorded in their books that the theory of the public interest was being substituted for the older doctrine of *laissez-faire*. . . . Presidents came and went, governors and legislatures came and went but the movement of social forces that produced this legislation was continuous. It was confined to no party, directed by no single organization, inspired by no over-powering leadership. Such were the processes and products of American democracy." [11]

By 1914, for Beard, the people had seized control of the nation. Tragically, however, Beard reported, during its moment of power, the American plutocracy had established a foreign policy of imperialism which was to lead the country into World War I. The plutocracy by 1890 argued that an American empire was necessary to absorb the surplus goods which they claimed were produced by American factories. And these men of power bent the Republican party to their will, forcing the political leaders to take America into economic competition for world markets. The peace-loving people, however, felt secure when Wilson became president because the

Democratic party had stood in critical opposition to this new policy of imperialism. But Wilson and many of the people, Beard wrote, were tricked by English propaganda into sympathy with the Allied cause. Wilson was also subjected to great pressure by eastern bankers and eastern intellectuals to support the Allies and finally, Beard declared, Wilson was seduced by his own ambition to be a Messiah into betraying American isolation, and he plunged the country into a meaningless war.

When the war was over, the people reasserted their traditional view of foreign policy and rejected Wilson's policy of internationalism. The nation did not regain Jefferson's isolation in the 1920's, however, because the eastern plutocracy, grown still richer from war profiteering, controlled the Republican party and reinstituted a foreign policy of imperialism. Writing in the decade of normalcy, Beard had to admit that the future seemed dark. But he rejected Parrington's hopelessness. The common man was not corrupt. The enemy was not science, technology, and industrialism. The enemy was the alien, un-American, artificial aristocracy which had plagued the "people" since 1600. And the impersonal force of historical progress, now industrialism, was fated to restore rule by the producers.

Look closely at America in this era of Big Business, Beard wrote, and notice the hopeful signs of the coming democracy. For the first time, women were playing something like an equal role in the community. A new "spirit of charity, generosity, and benevolence" was abroad in the land. The social gospel spirit of progressivism was not dead but expanding; witness, he wrote, the great development of social work. Even the rich showed a new sense of responsibility, sharing their fortunes with the community to build better universities and laboratories and art galleries. And everywhere science gained in power and prestige — not the science of abstractions, but of utilitarianism that could be used to raise the standard of living of the people. American philosophy of the 1920's, of the machine age, was that of John Dewey, emphasizing the solution of specific social problems. Even more encouraging, throughout the social sciences there was criticism of that philosophy of determinism which had so frightened Parrington. The leaders of the social sciences understood the new physics which denied the existence of abstract absolutes. The social sciences were experimental and vital.

This vitality was also the hallmark of the arts and literature of the decade. Everywhere there was energy and experimentation related to the industrial philosophy of productivity. How long then could the plutocracy continue to rule a land of productive, democratic people? Let the people once recognize that America was progress, let them recognize that America "meant an invulnerable faith in democracy, in the ability of the undistinguished masses, as contrasted with heroes and classes . . . a faith in the efficacy of that new and mysterious instrument of the modern mind, 'the invention of invention,' moving from one technological triumph to another . . . effecting an ever wider distribution of the blessings of civilization . . . conjuring from the vasty deeps of the nameless and unknown creative imagination of the noblest order, subduing physical things to the empire of the spirit — doubting not the capacity of the Power that had summoned into being all patterns of the past and present, living and dead, to fulfill its endless destiny. If so, it is the dawn, not the dusk, of the gods." [12]

During 1928, 1929, and 1930, Beard's writings continued to emphasize the role of technology as the foundation of modern civilization and the necessarily democratic society that resulted from the workings of the machine process. He was trying to become the great educator of his people. He would teach them that they lived in two worlds, the world of fact and the world of imagination. The world of fact was that of technology and democracy; the world of imagination was that of capitalism and plutocracy. Americans did not realize that they lived in a world that could provide for everyone's material welfare because they were captives of the myths of English capitalistic economics. These false views had captured the minds of the business and university communities after the Civil War and dominated the press and clergy. This foreign ideology had been inculcated in the minds of the people so that they had lost sight of their democratic heritage as a cooperative community of producers. They were taught that they were prisoners of a set of iron economic laws which forced them to be competitive, to be acquisitive, which denied them the use of government as a tool for achieving community welfare through planning.

To reveal the reality of an American economy that was already cooperative and to a large extent planned, to prove the myth of *laissez-faire* and the falsity of antidemocratic theory, Beard published in 1930 another massive volume, *The American Leviathan*. Written in a cold, objective style, the book must have had, nevertheless, a prophetic ring during the first year of the great depression.

This book, Beard wrote, "is the result of an effort to unite politics, government, and technology as reflected in the federal system of the United

States, with emphasis on the newer functions created under the pressures of the machine age. . . . Natural science and machinery have set a new and complex stage for the operations of government, imposed additional functions upon it, and lifted it to a new role in the process of civilization." [13] Americans must understand, he continued, that society is a living whole and not an artificial construct of distinct and separate entities as English classical economics insisted. Government then is part of this social whole; it is not alien and hostile, a threat to the liberties of society. As part of society, it has the immensely important role of providing stability for society.

At a moment in American history when all stability seemed to be vanishing from the American economy, when people stood helpless before this terrible social disintegration, afraid to act because of their traditions which denied them the use of government in such an emergency, Beard became more than a purveyor of facts. Inevitably, his book became the basis of a new faith. If one believed Beard, this terrible economic crisis was not the end of the American dream; rather for the first time since Jefferson the dream could reach fulfillment. With capitalism smashed, democracy would emerge triumphant. The essence of democracy, Beard wrote, is a society governed by the people. Now ours, he continued, is a society marked by mass production and the people are the producers. The people, therefore, dominate. Mass production allows no aristocracy, no meaningful class divisions to appear. The government must work with the economic leaders to create a planned economy. Assuming a basically democratic society, Beard did not believe that there must be a revolution in the structure of the American economy. The only revolution needed was in the realm of ideas. Teach Americans that their philosophy of acquisitive individualism was an erroneous foreign ideology, teach them that the nature of society is cooperative, and they would cooperate. They would place national welfare above selfish interest. Business, agriculture, labor, and government were all natural parts of an organic society. Now, knowing the truth, they would work together.

In 1932, Beard advocated a "Five Year Plan for America." Here he argued that, because the inner logic of technology was rational planning, the modern idea of economic planning had been originated in the United States, the home of the technological revolution. It was Frederick W. Taylor, he wrote, who invented technological planning and the Russian Communists had borrowed the idea from him. Going back to Taylor for inspiration would help educate the people to planning which would preserve the best of the American tradition including private property but which "will lop off the dead wood of our futile plutocracy, so sinister in its influences on politics, culture, and rational living." The five-year plan was to be built around a National Economics Council in which the leaders of all the great industries were to come together to coordinate the economy and escape from the foreign ideology of cutthroat competition.[14]

This essay was published in 1932 in a book edited by Beard called *America Faces the Future*. By the end of 1933, Beard could announce to America that *The Future Comes*. In this volume, Beard analyzed the first revolutionary months of Franklin D. Roosevelt's administration and found them good because "The Recovery Program accepts the inexorable development of combination in industry, abandons all faith in the healing power of dissolution and prosecution; and makes use of combination in planning. . . . The Recovery Program calls upon millions of individuals in industry and agriculture, who have hitherto been pursuing their own interests at pleasure, to cooperate in adjusting production, setting prices, and maintaining standards — thus making imperative a new economic education on a colossal scale. The Recovery Program attacks the historic method of distributing wealth through the system of price and wage competition, and substitutes, in part at least, price and wage fixing. . . . Through its banking, credit, public-corporation, process-taxing, and railroad measures, the Recovery Program is moving in the direction of a new economic sequence which subjects private interests to a broad nationalization. . . . The New Deal signalizes [Beard concluded] the coming of a future collectivist in character." [15]

As Beard foresaw the collapse of capitalist plutocracy and the emergence of technological democracy, he came to feel that his role as educator to his people was not enough. Now that the cooperative commonwealth was re-emerging, it needed the humanization of a faith to make it complete. The people must rediscover their spiritual father, Thomas Jefferson. The European doctrines of classical *laissez-faire* and Marxism deny any spirituality to man. But an American faith will assert the spirituality of the world. This faith, he wrote, "will be simple at bottom, as simple as the Sermon on the Mount. . . . It will take the good life as its centre, for the plain reason that there is no other immovable bench mark in the universal flux. It will be planful, because the good life cannot be lived without scheme and control, and the supreme instrumentality of our age, engineering, is planful in operation. . . . It must be valid whatever varieties of religious faith may prevail, and must command the assent of multitudes, who differ in religious belief. It must find its sanctions in society itself." [16]

Beard clarified this earthly faith and its relationship to technology in a preface he wrote in 1932 to J. B. Bury's *The Idea of Progress*. After praising Bury for discovering that the idea of progress had been the dominant faith for the last two centuries, he criticized the Englishman for suggesting that this faith would pass. Bury, Beard argued, did not take into account the fact that progress had become a faith because the development of technology in the eighteenth century had made progress a fact. "Bury suggests that the idea of progress may itself pass and be supplanted by another philosophy of history," Beard wrote, but he added that now we know that "there is something intrinsic in technology which seems to promise its indefinite operation." [17]

Progress then was a faith which could not fail because it was embodied in the factual essence of history. Beard made this faith and its impersonal factual context a unique part of American history. Born in Europe, the idea of progress was never fully accepted there by the common man who continued to accept the tyranny of the intellectuals committed to the values of the ancient past because of their classical educations. But America was populated by lower-class Europeans who wanted to get ahead, who wanted progress, and American intellectuals were never really exposed to a classical education. Only in America did progress become a national faith and a fact of life. But, Beard added, one can never prove the existence of social facts as one proves the existence of the facts of natural science. Ultimately, one must accept social facts on faith as values. Progress was a fact and a value; it was objective and a faith. For Beard, "the idea of progress is both an interpretation of history and a philosophy of action."

This is the view that Beard tried to explain in his presidential address to the American Historical Association in December 1933, "Written History as an Act of Faith." He began with the firm assertion that the only meaningful definition of history is that it is what historians think about the past. This thought is based upon empirical knowledge about the past "authenticated by criticism and ordered by the help of the scientific method" but its fundamental patterns do not emerge from the facts, from criticism, or from the scientific method. Rather, Beard argued, the basic structure of our writings reflects our philosophy of history because ultimately each historian selects a particular set of facts about the past which he calls representative. As philosophers rather than scientists, Beard continued, we are not caught, however, in meaningless relativity. There are only three possible philosophies of history. There is, first, the philosophy that history has no meaning and no one can possibly write history who holds to this view of history as chaos. Secondly, one can believe that history is marked by cycles and man is doomed to the endless tragedy of meaningless repetition of the past. And finally one can believe that history is progress. No self-respecting historian, Beard declared, will accept the idea that history deals with meaningless cycles of human behavior. Historians must write history from the perspective of an idea of progress. They must have faith that there is progress and they must fulfill that faith. My own theory of progress, he concluded, is in the emergence of a "collectivist democracy" in America.[18]

Meanwhile Beard was becoming increasingly concerned with the only major factors that he believed could check progress: imperialism and internationalism. By appealing to patriotism, the reactionary forces of the plutocracy might be able to lead the people into foreign adventures which would block progress at home and allow the alien aristocracy to regain control of the country.

To check this conspiracy, Beard directed his energy into the writing of two books, *The Idea of National Interest* and *The Open Door at Home,* both published in 1934, which were to educate the people to this peril and give them the inspiration and faith to rise above it. Foreign policy today, Beard began his argument in *The Idea of National Interest*, is the expression of what people consider their national interest. What then is the real national interest of the American people that must be expressed in the country's present and future foreign policy?

One tradition of national interest, he wrote, that had dominated national foreign policy was begun by Hamilton; it was the foreign policy of the Federalist, Whig, and Republican parties. It assumed American prosperity depended upon the expansion of foreign markets for the nation's industrial and agricultural surplus. The leaders of this policy had no concern for the uniqueness of the American republican experiment. They were willing to corrupt American innocence through the creation of an empire and by "bringing in immigrants still less adapted to the national heritage than many races later excluded by law, thus adding to the confusion of peoples, the babel of tongues . . . already existing in the country."[19] No one has ever been able to demonstrate, Beard continued, that this policy is based on economic truth. Indeed, all evidence points to the conclusion that if American production were distributed throughout the community by intelligent economic planning, there would be national prosperity without foreign markets.

Beard next described the equally fallacious policy of internationalism held by the Jeffersonian Republican and Democratic parties. But for Beard, Jefferson, unlike Hamilton, was not to blame for this erroneous tradition of the parties he helped create. Jefferson, Beard made clear, was no internationalist. He "was a nationalist in a narrow and racial sense, and looked to the development, on this continent, of a homogeneous people primarily engaged in agriculture — a society of people speaking a common language, knit together by ties of blood and language, capable of self-government, and so placed in a strategic geographical position as to be easily defended without large military and naval establishments — those historic menaces to liberty." [20] Jefferson's followers, however, concerned with marketing their agricultural products abroad, became internationalists and accepted the ideology of *laissez-faire*. As the Hamiltonians assumed a world of war in which the United States must compete, the Democrats came to assume a world of peace in which the United States must cooperate.

Indeed, Beard agreed, the world outside the United States was one of disharmony and war but the country did not have to participate in this foreign chaos. Secure on its own continent, the nation, with only enough military might to defend the Western hemisphere, should develop its own economy and absorb the so-called surpluses in industry and agriculture in an expanding standard of living. This, he affirmed, is the only valid national interest.

In these years between 1929 and 1934, the years of the great economic disaster, people had proof of the inadequacies of these two traditional views of national interest. As the new president had recognized the bankruptcy of the old economic order at home and the need for a New Deal, so there was evidence that he saw the need for a new foreign policy. Central to his outlook in 1933 was the idea that "by domestic planning and control the American economic machine may be kept running at a high tempo supplying the intranational market, without relying primarily upon foreign outlets for 'surpluses' of goods and capital." And yet, Beard complained, Roosevelt continued building the navy as if it would be used for international war rather than continental defense. Why did not the president adjust concrete policy to his new philosophy? This was the urgent question that ran through the last pages of Beard's book. Was the president unaware of how revolutionary his new outlook was? Was he unaware that he could play the role of a Moses to his people, leading them out of the desert of outmoded ideas? Roosevelt, Beard asserted, must lead a revolution to overthrow the imperialism of the Republican party and the internationalism of the Democratic party and restore the continental policy of Jefferson.

The Open Door at Home, the sequel to *The Idea of National Interest*, is an enthusiastic description of the Jeffersonian covenant and a stirring appeal to the American people to recognize their special role in history as a chosen people and to accept their responsibility to preserve and extend their uniquely democratic tradition by isolating themselves from the corrupting influence of the Old World.[21]

But by 1935, this message of necessary isolation for American democracy had changed from a prophecy of the coming people's republic to a warning of impending doom. The great democratic leader, Franklin Roosevelt, had refused to adjust his foreign policy to his philosophy of economic nationalism. He continued the Republican policy of hostility to Japan and of building a navy to challenge Japanese power in the Far East. With deep despair, Beard predicted that Roosevelt would probably lead the country into war against Japan. And he suggested that Roosevelt might have defected from reform to become a defender of the plutocracy and was about to try to save the vested interests from radical reconstruction of the economy at home by beginning a foreign adventure that would lead the people away from democracy.[22]

Beard, however, had not yet surrendered hope. He still thought it useful to send his essays on foreign policy to President Roosevelt. A man committed to industrial democracy at home could not be a fully corrupted agent of international finance-capitalism. When Beard published *America in Midpassage* in 1939 as the sequel to his *Rise of American Civilization,* it was not completely surprising that Franklin D. Roosevelt emerged as the hero of this decade of transition. Beard still hoped to redeem the president.

In six hundred detailed pages, Beard related the confusing patterns of economics, politics, and foreign policy between 1927 and 1937. It was clear from his lack of emphasis and the absence of sharp generalization that Beard was not as sure as he had been in 1933 that the old order of the 1920's had given way to a "New Deal." But in his last four hundred pages, which dealt with the cultural life of the nation, Beard did find clear-cut evidence of the increasing victory of democratic vigor over aristocratic decadence. Here, in American cultural life, there was a New Deal. Notice, wrote Beard, the vitality of the Federal Theater project. Notice the renaissance of American art under government sponsorship. The people, at last, are learning that they are social members of an organic community. "Primitive art had expressed communal organization and purpose. . . . Now, through the patronage of the arts by the government of the United States, art was again to be a public affair. . . . [the artist again communed] with the people at large — the fountain-head of democratic government." [23]

If this democratic resurgence in the arts could be blended with a democratic resurgence in science, then, Beard wrote, the cultural stage would be set for the total definition of American society by American ideals. Then all the poisonous, pernicious, undemocratic doctrines from Europe would be discarded and American civilization would stand forth as a beacon of light in a world of darkness. And this fusion of an American art and science was taking place. Scientists, Beard proclaimed, were discovering that man, not mechanical law, was the measure of value.

With this blending of art and science, of theory and practice, of ideal and reality, the tragic dualism of American culture was being ended and organic unity achieved. The first great practitioner of this cultural organicism was Franklin D. Roosevelt, who "combined in his thinking, the severe economic analysis of the Hamilton-Webster tradition with the humanistic democracy of the parallel tradition. . . . In his second inaugural he took cognizance of the fundamental . . . antithesis between the ideal and the real . . . and having accepted this conflict as a challenge, President Roosevelt expressed the conviction that it was the function of statesmanship to bring the real into closer conformity to the ideal — the conception of humanistic democracy. . . . It was well within the circle of factual description to say that in his numerous discourses Franklin D. Roosevelt discussed the basic human and economic problems of American society with a courage and range displayed by no predecessor in his office . . . that he . . . stirred the thought of the nation to the uttermost borders of the land. And in doing this he carried on the tradition of humanistic democracy which from colonial times had been a powerful dynamic in the whole movement of American civilization and culture — economic, political, literary, scientific and artistic." [24]

Beard believed he had come this close to his goal. By 1938, Americans had discovered the reality of an organic society and a man great enough to provide it leadership. But by 1939, this man of destiny was destroying the promise of American life; he was delivering America into the hands of a corrupt and decadent Europe. Desperately, in two books, *Giddy Minds and Foreign Quarrels* and *A Foreign Policy for Americans*, Beard attempted to rally the people against Roosevelt's policy of internationalism. He reassured them that the vast majority of their neighbors wanted to stay aloof from Europe's wars and if this majority stood firm, it could block the machinations of any evil man.[25]

Beard's last major book before America's entry into World War II was a terrifying description of the totalitarian state built up by Roosevelt. Trying to find ways of checking Roosevelt's power of leadership, Beard now abandoned his earlier estimate of the New Deal. More drastically, he abandoned his theory of the organic community which he had held at the end of the 1920's and throughout the formative years of the New Deal. Beard's first book about the New Deal had been *The Future Comes*. Now in 1940 his title *The Old Deal and the New* symbolized Beard's thesis that the so-called New Deal was only a continuation and consolidation of the old. But in spite of this thesis, Beard did emphasize the novelty of the New Deal. Under the old deal, the people had been ruled by a plutocracy; under the New Deal, they were ruled by a dictatorship. In 1933, Beard had praised Roosevelt's dynamic leadership. In 1940, he damned the people for their passive acceptance of that leadership: "Never in all the history of the country, not even during the long Civil War, had the people moved in such an intellectual and emotional daze as they did while these events transpired. In their easy, almost abject, acceptance of all that was handed out to them by the Administration was revealed a profound change in national temper — a deeper subservience to government policy and instruction." [26]

In 1933, Beard had praised Roosevelt for preserving the existing structures in industry, banking, and agriculture through governmental aid in order to use them as the basis for a planned economy under governmental coordination. This was the organic society. Now Beard in 1940 damned Roosevelt for planning a dictatorship by making the economy dependent on the national government: "Having failed to take their heavy liquidation in 1932 and 1933 and to manage successfully 'their own affairs' economic and political, the private interests and the state and local political interests, which had once exercised powerful checks on the power and momentum of the Federal Government, lost a large part of their independence;

and, as Congress escaped its responsibilities by transferring to the Executive a huge discretionary authority in relation to banking, currency, and spending, centralization proceeded rapidly. In this way the old system of checks and balances, political and economic, was profoundly altered." [27]

Beard had dramatically ended his personal tradition of viewing the Constitution and the Supreme Court as the chief sources of protection for the corporation, that alien institution, through which the eastern aristocracy planned to dominate the people. For three decades, he had urged that the power of the presidency and Congress be increased and liberated from the restraints of the Constitution and the Supreme Court because he saw these agencies as representative of the will of the people. Through them, the spontaneous power of the people could be channeled along a course which would shatter the control of the corporation and free the economy. When Beard now suddenly defined the presidency and Congress as themselves institutionalized power, infiltrated by the eastern establishment, he cried out for a return to the philosophy of checks and balances and limited government presided over by the Supreme Court which had been propounded by the founding fathers. Beard summarized this new viewpoint in 1943 when he published *The Republic*.

In his last major work, *President Roosevelt and the Coming of the War 1941*, which appeared in 1948, Beard gave the people an object lesson in the importance of limited constitutional government. The people had abdicated their responsibility to constitutional government in the 1930's; they had given the president the power of a tyrant. Although the average American did not want war, President Roosevelt was able, because of his control of institutionalized power, to maneuver the country into a foreign war. Judge Roosevelt by the standards of the Constitution, Beard demanded, and he stands revealed as an immoral man, a man who was able to use evil means to achieve evil ends because the people had not jealously guarded their constitutional rights of a government of checks and balances. [28]

But even in the 1940's, after the coming of a war that Beard had warned would end American democracy, he refused to be the defeated Jeremiah that Parrington had been in 1927. Beard still promised his people that if they repented and went back to the old faith, history was on their side. The covenant still lived. "Calamities may come upon America or be brought upon the country by demagogic leadership. Civil storms may shake the United States. Temporary dictatorships may be set up. [But] . . . Enough of our Republic will be kept intact to restore, rebuild, and go ahead." [29] This was the inspiring message of Beard's *The American Spirit* of 1942, the last volume in his great survey of the American past which included *The Rise of American Civilization* and *America in Midpassage*. It set forth his final argument that the Jeffersonian covenant could not be destroyed, not even by the power of that massive economic institution, the corporation, or by the equally mighty political state.

America, Beard began, was born during the eighteenth-century Enlightenment and owes much to the European civilization of that time. The leaders of the Enlightenment fought to emancipate mankind from the tyranny of the Middle Ages and they developed the idea of progress. And the new American nation of 1789 was based on these principles of an emancipated mankind which could achieve infinite progress.

But, at this point, a major difference in ideas came to separate the leaders of the American Enlightenment from their European colleagues. Unique to the Americans like Jefferson, Beard wrote, was the idea of civilization. Jefferson assumed that because man was a social animal, the progressive community of emancipated men must be democratic and cooperative; that progress was not automatic but depended upon human will; that this will must be inspired by an ethical faith. Progress for Jefferson was a moral constraint, not a form of materialistic determinism as the Europeans believed. Jefferson, therefore, believed that the idea of civilization could serve as a national faith only in America because of the uniqueness of the American social harmony. Built on the new foundations of the frontier, America's origins, "unlike those of European societies, were not lost in pre-historic darkness, in mythological time, in the dim twilight of barbarism, pagan gods, superstitions, ignorance and fears." [30] By the 1830's this idea of democratic civilization, Beard continued, was producing a great renaissance of American culture. Emerson, Whitman, Margaret Fuller, and George Bancroft all gave artistic expression in diverse ways to the unique American destiny. All found their inspiration in the idea of a distinct American civilization. Even in economics, a man like Henry C. Carey expressed the uniqueness of American civilization, criticizing English classical economics for forgetting the Jeffersonian principles that man is an ethical animal and that history is a product of human effort.

These English economists had abstracted man from society, made him a prisoner of economic law, and argued that he was motivated only by selfishness. Now Beard began to trace the tragic decline of the Jeffersonian ideal as this English ideology infiltrated Jefferson's America. The American economy began to be dominated by bankers. They accepted the views of the English economists; then the bankers converted the American businessmen, whom they controlled, to this alien ideology; the businessmen in turn demanded that the college professors and the clergy, whom they controlled, teach this doctrine of acquisitive individualism. And by 1865, the official doctrine of America was English classical economics.

Beard provided a dramatic footnote to the power of this new "Establishment" by showing its control over two historians usually associated with Jeffersonianism, Woodrow Wilson and Frederick Jackson Turner. Both men, Beard related, thought they were Jeffersonians because they believed in the uniqueness of American civilization defined as individualism. Ironically, neither knew that they were defining America in terms of an English ideology.

But Beard asked his readers not to despair because almost immediately after the Civil War, Americans began to fight their way back to the real Jeffersonianism. Leaders in this movement were men like the anthropologist Lewis Henry Morgan, the sociologist Lester Frank Ward, the economists Simon Patten and Richard Ely, and the ministers of the social gospel Walter Rauschenbusch and George Herron. All defined man not only as naturally social and cooperative but also as progressive. All believed that history moved forward constantly, giving man the perpetual opportunity to improve his society. For the generation after 1900, however, young Americans would be deprived of these enduring truths by the diversion created by foreign critics of American civilization. These critics asked Americans to abandon the reality of the American experience and to lose sight of American uniqueness. Catholics asked our young people to look back to the ideal absolute of medieval theology; Marxists asked our youth to look forward to the ideal absolute of the Communist utopia.

Beard blamed the great influence of these doctrines for the failure of American historians to teach the reality of America. The Catholics and the Marxists were able to win young people by criticizing the selfish materialism of the United States. But, Beard asserted, acquisitiveness, the cash nexus, is not American; it is the result of English ideology. America, the real America, is the Jeffersonian concern for human cooperation, for the selfless ethic of true civilization. Working also to alienate the young people from the Jeffersonian covenant was the doctrine of internationalism propounded by men like "Louis Finkelstein under the title of 'American Ideals and the Survival of Western Civilization' in the *Contemporary Jewish Record* of June 1941." [31] It is no wonder, Beard wrote, that so many young intellectuals became cynical and pessimistic in the 1920's about their nation which was defined for them in terms of alien ideologies.

Beard had painted a scene of true moral drama. The good American intellectuals of the progressive era were locked in mortal combat with the evil representatives of European ideologies. Both sides were attempting to win the minds of young America. By 1920, the factor of American participation in the European war had seemed to give the advantage to the forces of darkness. Many promising young Americans were becoming expatriates. But even in this darkest hour of the Republic, the people, the sleeping giant, awoke to strike out in blind fury against its foreign corrupters. Beard found the beginning of the final victory of the forces of light in the national legislation restricting immigration: "Expressing in many respects this revulsion and this determination to protect American civilization against European and Oriental invasions, immigration legislation, especially the Acts of 1921 and 1924, stood out in public discussions and in law as positive testimony to renewed concentration on the reinforcement of civilization in the United States." [32] Now, said Beard, America was at last returning to the principles of the founding fathers. And once Americans began the rediscovery of their heritage, purged of foreign influence, their insights flourished in every area of cultural life.

Even the social scientists, Beard announced, were now escaping from bondage to English thought. The Commission of the Social Studies had issued in 1931 "A Charter for the Social Sciences," which declared that "America has never imported a large part of the Old World heritage. . . . Having rounded out the Continent, the American people have turned in upon themselves . . . the great body of thinkers still agree with Emerson that we must stand fast where we are and . . . build a civilization with characteristics sincerely our own." [33]

Beard then found this Jeffersonian continentalism to be the dominant philosophy among American thinkers in the 1930's, controlling political, economic, philosophical, and artistic thought, and he had hope. The American spirit, indeed, could not die; it was American history. Any contradictions to it were foreign intrusions, temporary parasitical growths, which could not permanently establish themselves here. "As to ultimates," Beard proclaimed, "while rejecting a total determinism, the idea of civilization predicates a partial determinism, such as an irreversible and irrevocable historical heritage, and a partially open and dynamic world in which creative intelligence can and does work; in which character can and does realize ethical values; in which virtue can and does make effective choices." [34]

Here indeed was a message of hope. Jeffersonianism could never be lost, it could only be improved. True American history could never be change but only progress because the foundation of American life was the rock of physical nature, not the ephemeral qualities of European institutions and traditions. And progress must be the restoration of the social simplicity of Jefferson's America.

Beard had denounced Europeans for holding to a materialistic view of history, for believing that human society was determined by material factors. Beard had affirmed that Americans were unique in their belief in man's freedom to shape his environment. Now he concluded his lifework by announcing that Americans were not free to destroy their Jeffersonian heritage because it had the eternal attributes of physical nature. Beard was expressing a theological tradition as old as George Bancroft — that in America God's spiritual purpose had found final and complete expression in the virgin land of the American frontier.

8 BECKER: THE COVENANT REPLACED BY CIVILIZATION

By THE END of the 1920's Beard, Becker, and Parrington had re-acted in different ways to the disintegration of the vision of a worldwide industrial millennium. Beard had salvaged the hope of national deliverance by rooting America's industrial future in the history of the agrarian frontier. But Becker and Parrington were not able to accept the view that industrialism was a frontier force destroying historical complexity and leading to natural simplicity. Rather they shared the nightmarish theory of Henry Adams that industrialism was bringing a crushing complexity which must inevitably destroy the individual. Parrington died a hopeless rebel against this theory he could not transcend. But Becker, by 1930, had constructed a philosophy of history which allowed him to ignore Adams' prophecy of impending doom. By retreating to the nominalism of the scientific historian of the nineteenth century, Becker was able to affirm that there were no patterns in history, only discrete facts. He might even pretend that the essence of the frontier hypothesis — the escape of the individual from the disharmony of the false traditions of historical society and the achievement of harmony with nature's truths — was fulfilled by the acceptance of this kind of scientific history. Nature's truths were meaningless facts but as long as one accepted these facts, one was free from the burden and responsibility of historical values.

But Becker could not finally accept this formula which might have provided a personal, if sterile, security. The closing pages of *The Heavenly City* revealed that Becker — however reluctantly — still believed that men and historians were part of history, were part of a changing society with changing values. He suggested there that the *philosophes*' religion of humanity still lived in the fighting Communist faith of contemporary Russia, that modern man was neither the cold, aloof scientist nor the historian, divorced from values, living by the facts, but the Communist, filled with faith in his cause and progress. And the Communists, like the men of the Enlightenment, were destined, therefore, to repeat history: "What, then, are we to think of all these 'great days,' these intimations of Utopia? Are we to suppose that the Russian Revolution of the twentieth century, like the French Revolution of the eighteenth, is but another stage in the progress of mankind toward perfection? Or should we think, with Marcus Aurelius, that 'The man of forty years, if he have a grain of sense, in view of this sameness has seen all that has been and shall be.' " [1]

Becker, like an Ernest Hemingway, yearned to make his separate peace and withdraw from a society which had lost its meaning. But for thirty years he had argued the social nature of the historian. In all intellectual honesty, he could not accept the myth of scientific history as tempting as it now was. In a review of Charles Beard's *The American Leviathan*, Becker had made clear his continuing belief in the social nature of man, a belief that now had become terrifying to a man who also believed so strongly in the freedom of the individual from social control: "With the best will in the world government can do little to change the character or the working of the complex social mechanism. It can't do much because it is not outside the mechanism. . . . It is itself a part of the machine. . . . The real Leviathan is not government, but society. . . . What can we do with it? Very little since we too are part of it. It carries us along whether we will or not. . . . We can at best play our part, perform our function, cultivate our gardens." [2]

This was the message Becker presented to the American Historical Association in his presidential address of December 1931. Against the setting of a Minnesota winter, he shared the chill of his defeated hopes with his colleagues. In a society that moves without direction, he declared, the historian must bravely pretend that his writings, which must quickly perish for want of truth, have meaning. Take heart, he said, because our only dignity comes from doing our jobs well; let us accept our responsibility as the "bards and story-tellers and minstrels" for our society.

Becker's address, "Everyman His Own Historian," succinctly sums up his view of the world and the historian's relation to it as of 1931. He began by telling his colleagues that there were two histories: the history of actuality and the history available to historians. This latter he defined as "the memory of things said and done." Next he emphasized the important role of this kind of history for "Mr. Everyman." Pointing out that everyone is in the process of facing tomorrow, he argued that the individual could not step into the future without an anticipation of what it would be like, an anticipation built on his memory of his own past history. Now, Becker lectured his fellow historians, it is clear that the individual's view of his own history and his own future is conditioned by the society in which he lives. He is not free to create any view of the past which he pleases; his historical vision must conform to that of his society. And, Becker argued, what is true of Mr. Everyman is true of the historian. The historian can discover only those historical patterns which his society has taught him to find; he selects only those facts which society tells him are important: "The history written by historians, like the history informally fashioned by Mr. Everyman, is thus a convenient blend of truth and fancy, of what we commonly distinguished as 'fact' and 'interpretation.' " [3]

Becker then tried to persuade his colleagues that they had not lost their dignity just because "Mr. Everyman is stronger than we are, and sooner or later we must adapt our knowledge to his necessities." We historians, he said, need worry no longer about the problem of values. "It should be a relief to us to renounce omniscience, to recognize that every generation, our own included, will, must inevitably, understand the past and anticipate the future in the light of its own restricted experience, must inevitably play on the dead whatever tricks it finds necessary for its own peace of mind." [4]

Becker was trying desperately to achieve peace of mind. In one year, he had found two means to this end. Both allowed the individual to throw off the burden of personal responsibility to any moral standard. Whether one defined the twentieth-century historian as the keeper of objective facts and matter-of-fact knowledge or as the servant of Mr. Everyman and the public policy, the historian escaped the burden of decision about what is good or evil, of having to work for the right and against the wrong.

How desperately Becker needed peace of mind, a way out of his dilemma as a liberal, is revealed in his textbook of 1931, *Modern History*, a survey of recent European history for high school students. Here Becker wrote as if he were still an enthusiastic advocate of the "new history"; he narrated a story of progress from the medieval past toward the liberal future. There are echoes of "Everyman His Own Historian" in a passage in his preface which reads: "The purpose of this book is to help you make this artificial extension of memory, help you stretch your memory over the last four hundred years, so that, by recalling the events that have occurred during that past time, you can more intelligently anticipate what is likely to occur during the years that are to come." [5] But Becker was not content with telling American high school students what was likely to occur; he also told them what should and must happen in the future if a democratic society was to survive. He wrote of the necessity of accepting the values of planning and internationalism, values which certainly did not meet with the approval of "Mr. Everyman" whom Becker was supposed to serve.

As Becker recounted the story of the development of modern Europe, the dynamic factors were science and technology. The industrial revolution and the extraordinary scientific and technological changes it brought created a vast new amount of wealth for society and made it possible for man to develop a humane outlook toward his fellow men. With material goods for everyone, mankind could afford the luxury of the ideals of equality and brotherhood. This democratic outlook was furthered, he wrote, by the necessary social and economic interdependence demanded by advancing technology.

This economic interdependence transcended national boundaries and led logically toward an international democracy as it had led to democracy within nations. Unfortunately, he continued, the doctrine of nationalism stood in the way of this trend and had ultimately brought world war. It was necessary, he concluded, for internationalism to replace nationalism as a value.

This was one crisis in values which must be resolved, Becker argued, but there was another. At the beginning of the nineteenth century, he wrote, men believed that political democracy solved all problems. By 1870, they began to become aware of the problem of social and economic democracy because a few men had gotten control of the vast new wealth created by the machines and this new aristocracy dominated the masses. The socialist movement challenged this situation and, in the name of democracy, urged distribution of the wealth coming from technology more equally throughout society by means of social and economic planning. And Becker agreed that social planning must be accepted if there was to be social peace, no war of classes, within a nation just as internationalism must be accepted if war between nations was to be avoided.

Becker's ultimate values were those of the eighteenth-century men who postulated that the goal of history was the free individual. And yet his intelligence told him that society would disintegrate into hellish anarchy and class warfare if there was no restraint on the individual, the restraint imposed by social and economic planning. In a deeply moving essay of 1932, "The Dilemma of Liberals in Our Time," Becker honestly, frankly, and publicly explored his inner conflict.

Liberalism, he began, the all-powerful position of a century ago, has lost its prestige. Why? Because, he wrote, its spokesmen argued that "every reasonable and virtuous man would follow his inclination and pursue his interest without interfering with the right of all other reasonable and virtuous men to do the same." But the industrial revolution put "a very great part of the wealth of the world in the hands, or at the disposal, of those persons, relatively few, who by intelligence, luck, or lack of scruple, managed to obtain control of the machines and the instruments of production; and accordingly . . . to give to the possessors of machines . . . a power over governments." Instead of the utopia promised by the eighteenth century, democracy has brought "political corruption, industrial brigandage, social oppression for the masses, and moral and intellectual hypocrisy on a scale rarely equaled and perhaps never surpassed." [6]

Can we liberals, Becker asked, wonder at the rapid development of socialism which has so effectively criticized the undemocratic world created in the name of democracy? Can liberals wonder at the demand of socialists for less liberty and more equality? Liberals are asked by the socialists and defenders of capitalism to choose: capitalism and liberty or socialism and equality. This is the dilemma of liberals whose democratic faith goes back to the Enlightenment, Becker continued, because we believe in both liberty and equality, "and the truth is that we cannot with clear convictions or a light heart have either without the other." If forced to choose, Becker admitted, he would probably choose liberty and he added that he would probably lose that liberty because the course of history was in the direction of equality. "What the average man wants," he wrote, "much more than he wants the liberties we prize, is security. . . . Uniformity, the equality of mediocrity, gives him all the liberty he needs. . . . And, unfortunately for us perhaps, the machines appear to be on the side of the average man." [7]

Then with surprising suddenness, Becker shifted the entire tone of the article from sardonic analysis to serious affirmation. Can we achieve equality in a humane and civilized fashion, he asked, avoiding the terrors of fascism and communism? He now argued that the greatest threat to the development of a sane policy of planning in America was an irrational commitment to liberty. Becker had begun this essay arguing the superior virtue of liberty; he ended it with an affirmation of the superior necessity of planning.

Becker obviously hoped that a form of democratic planning might yet achieve a balance between liberty and equality and avoid the totalitarian eradication of liberty as in fascism and communism. Intellectuals had an opportunity and a responsibility to shape history, he affirmed. They must act now in this economic crisis to stabilize and equalize the economy or democracy would be completely lost.

Was this sixty-year-old historian about to make a personal intellectual revolution and accept the burden of history? Would he continue to define the historian as one morally responsible for his society without the assurance of progress toward harmony and simplicity, as one whose task it was to balance freedom and equality in a confused and complex world?

Not surprisingly, Becker was once again to fight his way out of history, to re-establish briefly the faith of his youth, progress, and to avoid the problem of power. The progress he now offered his society was cold and hard. One came to this progress with stoic resignation, not joyful commitment. But it was still progress; like the old progress, it promised to take mankind out of confusion and complexity to a utopia of simplicity and harmony. It lifted the burden of moral responsibility from the individual and placed it within the historical process itself. Men did not have to decide what was good or evil; progress dictated to man what his values would be. Men would not have to be torn apart as they attempted to reconcile individualism and planning. History as progress made the choice inevitable — planning must replace liberty.

This was the theme of a series of lectures Becker delivered in 1936, which were published under the title *Progress and Power*. He began with a discussion of J. B. Bury's book on the idea of progress. He agreed with Bury that this idea had been the dominant religious faith of the last two centuries, though seriously weakened by the events of World War I. And he asked, "May we still, in whatever different fashion, believe in the progress of mankind?" In answer to his question, Becker now began a curious exercise in logic. We no longer have faith in progress, he argued; the idea of progress seems to depend upon human definition of desirable values and we do not see history moving toward the values we think are important.

But we must not think that there is no progress. One cannot define progress by the personal values of an individual or even a generation. The only way to define progress objectively is to see it in the perspective of the entire range of human history. If, in taking this overview of the entire record of mankind, we can observe a constant trend, a theme that unites the first prehistoric man with our present society, we can call this trend progress without judging it by our impermanent values. Becker solemnly assured his readers that he was now going to "dismiss all ethical and moral judgments, forget about the final or relatively good end toward which man may be moving, and endeavor to estimate human progress in terms of what man has in fact done, and of the means that have enabled him to do it." [8]

Let us begin, he declared, with a time scale that will represent the stages of human development. Let us agree that there have been men for approximately 506,000 years. The first period in the time scale lasted approximately 450,000 years, during which there was little change because men did not develop their sources of power; they continued with a few simple tools. But about 56,000 years ago, there was a breakthrough in the number of tools invented and used and a rapid change in the social structure, which became more cohesive. In this period of social growth, the social ideal was the small, homogeneous group in which there were no major distinctions between individuals; equality was the rule.

Then about 6000 years ago, Becker recounted, the third period of human history began. Its chief characteristic was the invention of writing, making possible records which would enlarge the imagination of man and increase his organizational capacity. With written records, man could vastly increase his knowledge of both time and space. When leaders were able to think in a regular fashion about time and space, it was possible for them to create great political empires which replaced the small social group as the nexus of human activity. Within the vast political state, specialization was a necessity and the ideal of social equality gave place to a hierarchy of individuals who ruled and were ruled in a state composed of sharply differentiated classes. Compared to the second period of human activity, this third age, the age of civilizations, made no notable advances in the invention of tools which gave man power over nature. Instead through the art of writing, the power of the barbarians — fire, the wheel, metal tools — was organized and systematized.

Indeed, Becker argued, the age of classic civilizations developed an imagination which stopped the growth of new sources of power. The leaders of the community came to see that the values of individuals, of societies, come and go: "There emerges the most devastating of all facts: Man, who alone knows and aspires, lives but a brief moment in an indifferent universe that alone endures." [9] Frightened, the leaders turned away from the mastery of material things to ask questions about the meaning of existence. They developed the great world religions in which the individual attempted to achieve harmony with a transcendent ideal. For them, the only reality was the life of the spirit.

But, Becker continued, within the medieval civilization of the West, there were practical men of affairs who, unlike the spiritual leaders, were concerned with mundane matters. These crude people were like the barbarians of the second period of evolution; they were new barbarians who would create the fourth and final period of history; they were the middle-class barbarians who discovered vast new sources of power by "losing interest in the manipulation of ideas through the medium of verbal symbols and becoming increasingly absorbed in the manipulation of things with the aid of mathematical concepts. . . . [They turned] with conscious purpose and systematic deliberation to the task of subduing the outer world of nature to human use." [10]

Becker was now about to rewrite radically the history of the eighteenth-century Enlightenment. In 1931, when he had lost confidence in progress, he described the Enlightenment as just another faith, a secularized version of medieval Christianity with no substantial basis in fact because, in 1931, Becker did not believe that facts pointed toward progress. In 1936, however, Becker again believed in progress as demonstrable fact. The *philosophes,* he now argued, had no relation to the Middle Ages. They were the complete antithesis of that period of esoteric imagination which asked unanswerable questions about irrelevant problems. The *philosophes* were the spokesmen for the emerging middle class who were "discovering a new, or rediscovering an old, technique for arriving at truth . . . following their practical interests, they accept the verdict of experience, and thereby extend the realm of matter-of-fact to include the entire outer world of things and the intangible forces that are in and behind appearance. For the revealed story of the life of man they will substitute a verified account of the factual experience of men. . . . We can see . . . that they are dispensing with the assistance of the gods in the effort to find out for themselves what man has in fact done (History), how things do in fact behave (Science). . . . Thus there emerges within the European climate of opinion . . . the idea of human Progress." [11]

The history of man, Becker wrote, is the history of man's progress in achieving power over nature. For 500,000 years, this describes man's activities. Then for almost 6000 years, men retreated into their own minds and tried to achieve harmony with a spiritual world that they created out of their imaginations. This brief interlude was ending by 1600 and was over by 1700 when modern men became conscious of what their real history had been, the conquest of nature. Yes, Becker continued, the *philosophes* had faith in progress but it was a mundane faith that grew out of reality; it was radically different from the spiritual faith of the medieval past.

During the classical period, men believed that the good life for man was to be found in a lost Golden Age or in a Heaven after death. Now the *philosophes* defined the good life as "the progressive amelioration of man's earthly state by the application of his intelligence to the mastery of the outer world of things and to the conscious and rational direction of social activities." [12] By 1800, Becker continued, men were able to visualize a utopia in which the machines would free all men from the burden of labor and provide the leisure necessary to well-rounded personality development. The history of Western man from 1800 to the present has been marked, however, by constant disappointment. Knowing that history is progress, men wondered anxiously why progress had not been fulfilled. Becker could now answer this question.

It is scientists and engineers who revolutionize the amount of power available to men but they do not distribute that power: "Within an industrial society of uprooted and freely competing individuals, in which wealth replaces birth and occupation as the measure of power and prestige, there emerge certain individuals, favored above others by intelligence and opportunity, who acquire control of the new implements of power, appropriate the surplus wealth created by them. . . . the new power discovered by scientists and mediated by engineers is placed at the disposal of the few." [13]

At first glance, Becker added, it might seem easy for the scientists and engineers to enlist the support of the masses, who live in poverty in the midst of potential plenty, to overthrow the selfish aristocracy and liberate the full productivity of science and technology. But this has been the tragedy of the last century. The scientific elite lives in the fourth and final period of history: "The exceptional few move with assurance and live at ease in an infinitely expanded time-and-space world. The matter-of-fact knowledge which enables them to supply common men with new and exciting implements of power enables them also to dispense with traditional views of the origin, the character, and the destiny of man. For them it is possible without distress to contemplate man as a biological organism that has slowly, through countless ages, emerged. . . . it is possible without strain to adjust their ethical judgments and social habits to the pragmatic implications of this enlarged time-and-space frame of reference." [14] But the average man still lives in the third period, the medieval world of myth with "a mass intelligence that functions most effectively at the level of primitive fears and tabus." Consequently, the selfish plutocracy has been able to manipulate the masses against their best interests while the scientists have not been able to communicate with them and lead them in the direction of their welfare, in the direction of progress.

Let us not despair, however, Becker declared; the course of history, of progress, is irreversible. Matter-of-fact knowledge will necessarily increase in spite of the political irrationality of the plutocracy and the masses: "Is it then too much to expect that in time to come it will be extended to include the world of human relations. . . . The machines, not being on the side of the angels, remain impassive in the presence of indignation, wishful thinking, and the moral imperative, but respond without prejudice or comment or ethical reservation to relevant and accurate knowledge while dismissing value judgments as useless or insufficiently discriminated." [15]

Becker had seemed to cut the Gordian knot of the eighteenth century: how to reconcile liberty and equality. To enlighten his fellow liberals of the 1930's, he demonstrated that liberty was important to the *philosophes* because they needed to destroy the false authority of medieval traditions and institutions. The *philosophes* had wanted liberty to free the human mind from myth; they wanted the mind to be free to discover the laws of nature. Then they wanted men to conform to the laws of nature. And the laws of nature pointed to the equality of man, not the equality of the myth-bound common man, but the equality of man guided by the matter-of-fact knowledge of science, technology, and the machine. Liberty was a tool to achieve equality. There was no longer a dilemma for liberals. Equality was not a value to choose and support. It was a necessary fact to accept and adjust to; it was the law of nature, of evolution, of progress.

Desperately rethinking the meaning of human history, Becker seemed to have finally escaped from Adams' prophecy that the evolution of science and technology was leading mankind to its doom. Placing his previous attitudes within his new perspective, he wrote that he had expected progress to culminate in a millennium in 1918, that he had reacted in a childlike fashion to the destruction of his dream. But now he was aware that progress was a process that continued over endless centuries. Certainly there were local disasters which interrupted the straight-line march of progress, but always the advance of science and technology continued. If its course was not constantly smooth, it was nevertheless inexorable.

There was to be a final irony in Becker's intellectual odyssey. Having at last constructed an interpretation of history which allowed him to regain the faith of his youth, he now, with the beginning of World War II, was to turn his back resolutely on the frontier tradition. In the last years of his personal history, he was to begin a great adventure in ideas by embracing that idea of history from which he had fled all his life. He was to reject the idea that history was a progression which was emancipating mankind from the complexities of civilization and leading men into harmony with natural principles. The dignity of man, Becker was to affirm, is found in accepting the responsibility of defending traditions of the past, not in destroying them. Becker was to appeal to Americans to abandon isolation in order to defend the values that gave essential meaning to their lives, values which were rooted deep in the history of the Old World and which linked the United States to its parent civilization in Europe.

This fundamental revolution in ideas is revealed in Becker's book of essays, *New Liberties for Old*, published in 1941. It contains a major essay for each year between 1936 and 1941.

The essay of 1936, "New Liberties for Old," captures the essence of Becker's commitment to the frontier tradition of hostility to history. Here Becker criticized all modern political thought for its failure to transcend history. The emerging democratic thought of the seventeenth and eighteenth centuries he damned as a continuation of medieval tradition and a rationalization of bourgeois institutions. Since 1850, Becker continued, this liberal democratic ideology has been gradually replaced by Marxism as the dominant faith of modern man. Like liberal democracy, Marxism was also a secularized version of the Christian tradition and a rationalization of class interest. When Becker wrote in 1936 that, "Looked at in the long perspective of human history, the liberal and communist ideologies are seen to be different formulations of the modern doctrine of progress, which is itself scarcely more than a secularization of the Christian doctrine of salvation," [16] he was relegating both doctrines to the ash heap of history. We must, he argued, escape from ideology to matter-of-fact knowledge, from history to nature: "One may suppose then that in the future . . . the realm of the matter-of-fact apprehension of experience may be so greatly extended that the effective social ideology will take on the flexible, pragmatic character of a scientific hypothesis." [17]

In his essay of 1937, "Loving Peace and Waging War," Becker was still concerned with the destruction of ideology, but his emphasis had shifted. He was concerned with myths of modern history rather than irrelevant faiths from the medieval past. Man, he argued, is competitive because of his biological inheritance. This aspect of human nature must be controlled if war is to be avoided. Instead modern civilization has unleashed and encouraged the warlike instincts of man. From Machiavelli on, we have believed that one nation can gain by the defeat of another. We have ignored not only the moral unity of civilization but also its economic unity. Therefore, World War I brought both moral and economic disaster to the victorious as well as to the vanquished nations. With anguish and frustration, Becker asked how it was possible to escape this vicious tradition of national competition when all the Western nations teach the value of competition either by individuals or by classes. Becker had shifted from his lifelong affirmation that harmony was to be achieved by escaping from historical society to a new affirmation that harmony must be re-created within the existing society. Suddenly Becker, who had interpreted constitutions as the expressions of ephemeral tradition and class interest, discovered that constitutions were necessary instruments to achieve social harmony.

In 1938, commenting on the one hundred and fiftieth anniversary of the American Constitution, Becker entitled his essay "After Thoughts on Constitutions." He began by noting that the great age of constitution-making between 1775 and 1875 had been based on a naive faith that political utopias could be established by discovering the natural rights of man and guaranteeing their expression in constitutions. In 1938, Becker did not disavow his connection with this naive faith as he had in 1936. Instead he described himself as part of a generation brought to a tragic dilemma: "What confuses our purposes and defeats our hopes is that the simple concepts upon which the Age of Enlightenment relied with assurance have lost for us their universal and infallible quality. Natural law turns out to be no more than a convenient and temporary hypothesis. Imprescriptible rights have such validity only as prescriptive law confers upon them. Liberty, once identified with emancipation of the individual from governmental restraint, is now seen to be inseparable from the complex pattern of social regulation. Even the sharp, definitive lines of reason and truth are blurred. Reason, we suspect, is a function of the animal organism, and truth no more than the perception of discordant experience pragmatically adjusted for a particular purpose and for the time being." [18] Candidly, Becker now affirmed his support for constitutionalism in spite of these intellectual difficulties. It was an affirmation without pretense: "We still hold . . . to the belief that man can, by deliberate intention and rational direction, shape the world of social relations to humane ends. We hold to it, if not from assured conviction, then from necessity, seeing no alternative except cynicism or despair." [19]

By 1939, when he wrote "When Democratic Virtues Disintegrate," it was clear that Becker was engaged in a major rethinking of his theory of history. He had become convinced that men must act to end the anarchy of the modern world. The philosophy of individual, class, and national competition must be replaced by a social philosophy of cooperation between individuals, classes, and nations within constitutional limitations on tyrannical power. For America, Becker wrote, the immediate problem at home was to achieve economic stability. If we are to preserve those virtues which are the basis of constitutionalism — tolerance, moderation, good will, rationality — then we must provide economic well-being for the mass of the community. This means economic planning. If we are to go forward to a planned economy, Becker continued, we must get rid of our frontier attitude: "The pragmatic American temper may . . . become a liability if the economic crisis deepens and is prolonged. . . . Confronted with a crisis that does not readily yield to the improvised short cut, the easy optimism with which we commonly ignore unpleasant truths and dismiss theories as of 'no use in practice' may very well prove a serious handicap. Our disposition then would be to regard unpleasant truths as heresies." [20]

Becker was certainly a moralist, a preacher, by 1940. But he was not a Jeremiah in the tradition of the American historian. He was trying to lead Americans away from the Jeffersonian covenant, trying now to take them back into history to find their values in a past which preceded the American frontier. If America must give up its frontier tradition and accept social planning, if Americans must believe in constitutionalism but in a constitution which changes through time, then it was crucial to establish the existence of values in society and in history. Here is the meaning of his essay of 1940, "Some Generalities That Still Glitter." The philosophical justification of democracy, he began, is a belief in the rationality of man. And yet for a century, the intellectual history of Western civilization has been hostile to this concept. The trend of philosophy in the nineteenth century was toward historical relativism. "To understand an idea it was then, above all, necessary to relate its history, and so identify it as thirteenth century or eighteenth century. . . . In this climate of opinion, the cardinal doctrines of the democratic faith could be most conveniently apprehended as an ideology in relation to the conflicts of a bygone revolutionary age." [21] Becker, who confessed his part in the intellectual irresponsibility of historical relativism, now pointed to another area of cultural irresponsibility in which he had also participated, the cult of technology — "The incessant preoccupation with machines and the machine process, which confirmed common men in a native disposition to take a literal and pragmatic view of life. . . . Modern man . . . is enamored of mechanical force. Fascinated by the delicate precision and sheer power of the devices he has invented, he is disposed to use them for doing whatever by their aid can be done, in the confident expectation that what can be done with such clean efficiency must be worth doing." [22] And this doctrine, Becker concluded, led directly to the acceptance of the doctrine that whatever is, is right, to the conclusion that might makes right. Now we must reaffirm that reason exists, he declared, that human values exist. We must find evidence of this reason and these values in history, not the history of particular times and places but the history of civilization: "To have faith in the dignity and worth of the individual man as an end in himself, to believe that it is better to be governed by persuasion than by coercion, to believe that fraternal good will is more worthy than a selfish and contentious spirit. . . . these are values which are affirmed by the traditional democratic ideology. But they are older and more universal than democracy and do not depend upon it. They have a life of their own apart from any particular social system." [23]

Becker clarified this idea of civilization in his final essay, that of 1941, "The Old Disorder in Europe." Here he described Nazi dictatorship as a return to Oriental despotism. Hitler's vision of a new order was based on concepts of political absolutism, of coercion, regimentation, and military imperialism, which were foreign to European civilization. The authentic European tradition he traced to Roman law and Christian ethics; it was upon these principles that a concept of constitutionalism became central to European civilization in the Middle Ages. The weakness of medieval constitutionalism, Becker continued, was that the community had no political means to impose restraint upon a king who attempted to subvert the constitution. But, Becker found, "This essential weakness was remedied by the liberal-democratic revolution which occurred from the seventeenth to the nineteenth centuries. The revolution reaffirmed the ancient maxim that political authority derives from law and law from the consent of the people. . . . It endeavored, mainly through written constitutions, to define more precisely and guarantee more effectively the limits of governmental power and the realm of individual rights within which citizens were free to speak and act without fear of arbitrary political interference." [24] European civilization collapsed, however, in 1914, Becker concluded, because of its failure to achieve economic justice; a philosophy of economic selfishness ultimately led to war. Out of this chaos grew the negative philosophy of Nazism which was attempting to destroy all order, all values. Becker was now preparing the philosophical justification for America's participation in a war against Nazi Germany. America must fight to conserve the European order of which it was a part. Certainly, America and Europe needed reform; the fatal weaknesses of economic and intellectual irresponsibility that had brought civilization to the horror of 1914 and of 1939 must be done away with. But, he warned, the immediate problem is the conservation of that which is good in this civilization.

In 1941, Becker published a small book, *Modern Democracy,* which summarized this developing philosophy. Here was his great effort to teach his fellow Americans to see their democracy with new eyes. They must learn that democratic values are those of Western civilization and are as enduring as that civilization. They must accept community responsibility for finding the right institutional means for expressing those values. There has to be community planning because democratic values need a precise economic and social environment to flourish. Without economic and social justice, political and intellectual democracy cannot exist. Americans have not understood the necessary relationship between the ideals of democracy and economic and social conditions because they have been prisoners of the eighteenth-century philosophy of progress. They had believed in the possibility of the self-sufficient individual because they had expected the appearance of a naturally harmonious society when all medieval institutions were destroyed.[25]

Becker dramatized the American failure to recognize the necessary social environment of man in an essay of 1943, "What Is Still Living in the Political Philosophy of Thomas Jefferson." Here Becker declared that "In all that relates to the fundamental values of life, both for the individual and for society, in all that relates to the ideal aims that democratic government professes to realize, [Jefferson's] understanding was profound. But in respect to the means, the particular institutional forms through which these values and ideal aims were to be realized, he was often at fault." [26] Jefferson's failure, the American liberal failure, the European liberal failure, was caused by an inability to see the continuing involvement of the individual in a society being revolutionized by industrialism. Jefferson and the American and European liberal, fearing power, avoided the problem of its responsible use by postulating an eternally simple society where power did not and would not exist. But, Becker warned, if democratic liberalism is to continue to exist, it must accept the reality of power, the inevitability of power, and use it to bring reform at home and in the world.

How well Becker understood the reluctance of American liberals to accept the inevitable existence of power and the responsibility for using it! From 1900 to 1936, his historical theories had always allowed Carl Becker to avoid responsibility for power. Now with the acceptance of power and his responsibility for it, he achieved a remarkable poise and assurance in his writing. Perhaps they came from the certainty he had achieved in the realm of values. Perhaps he could accept the responsibility for power because he no longer defined himself as a solitary individual. He saw himself as a participant in a great tradition; he spoke with the authority of that tradition. He found the burden of history easier to carry than that of the frontier covenant which had isolated him and his contemporaries from previous generations of mankind.

Becker had clearly surrendered the frontier covenant and its peculiar burden of innocence when he published in 1944 *How New Will the Better World Be*. This was a book designed to save American liberals from reliving the intellectual disaster of 1919. Arguing the inescapable continuity of history, it began with a quotation from Edmund Burke: "Society is indeed a contract. . . . But the state ought not to be considered as nothing better than a partnership agreement . . . to be taken up for a little temporary interest, and to be dissolved by the fancy of the parties. . . . It is a partnership . . . in every virtue, and in all perfection. And as the end of such a partnership cannot be obtained in many generations, it becomes a partnership not only between those who are living, but between those who are living, those who are dead, and those who are to be born." [27]

We Americans must reform the world, Becker wrote. Of this there can be no question if we are to avoid repeating World War II. The basic reform needed is an international order which can remove or control the causes of war. Central to such an order is economic planning and America must begin economic planning at home before it can play a role in international planning. But first of all Americans must be educated into the basic economic reality of their civilization: industrialism, which has created a permanent revolution for the United States and the entire world. Before they can comprehend the existence of this permanent revolution, Americans must be taught to see the fallacy of the tradition that the United States is outside of historical change. Our citizens cannot be so educated until their educators learn that utopia is not possible. Before World War I, Becker argued, American intellectuals accepted the necessity of economic planning at home and international planning abroad, and they expected domestic and international "progressivism" to usher in an immediate utopia. They were cruelly disillusioned by the experience of World War I and withdrew from intellectual leadership. They allowed "progressivism" to collapse and "normalcy" to reassert itself. Now the great depression and World War II have revived both domestic and international "progressivism." Becker pleaded with his fellow intellectuals not to expect the war to end in a millennium. They must not be disillusioned again. They must accept the necessity and responsibility of the continuing use of power during peacetime to move toward a piecemeal achievement of their ideals.

Let us end this war with our eyes open, he asked of his fellow intellectuals. Let us gain strength and courage and dignity from that unbroken civilization of which we are the latest leaders. Let us recognize that "With those who are dead we have maintained this partnership by cherishing what they have bequeathed to us. With those who are living we are maintaining it by fighting to preserve our inheritance from destruction. With those who are to be born we shall maintain it if, besides passing this legacy on to them, we can make such additions to its accumulated store of knowledge and wisdom as our generation is capable of producing." [28]

Carl Becker had presented Americans with a new interpretation of history. History was not progress from institutional and traditional complexity to natural simplicity. History was the record of man's moral responsibility to preserve civilization in its necessarily complex expression in constantly changing institutions and traditions.

9 DANIEL BOORSTIN: BLACKSTONE AND THE CONSERVATION OF THE AMERICAN COVENANT

DECEMBER 7, 1941, the Japanese attack on Pearl Harbor, marks one of the great turning points in American history. From 1789 to 1940, the official diplomatic policy of the nation was one of no entangling alliances. It was a policy that found its philosophic support in the Jeffersonian covenant. From Bancroft to Beard, historians had justified the necessary isolation of the emerging nation on the grounds that the United States represented a new civilization. Ours was a fragile culture of infinite purity and perfection, the historians argued, and must not be endangered by contamination from abroad. Now in the years after 1941, the diplomatic policy of America was to be revolutionized through the making of military alliances with the nations of western Europe and southeastern Asia. In the postwar world, the United States seemed permanently committed to defending its interests in every area of the world — Europe, Asia, Africa, and South America.

It appeared then that the dramatic intellectual conflict in 1941 between Charles Beard's defense of the Jeffersonian covenant and Carl Becker's rejection of the tradition of American uniqueness had been resolved in Becker's favor by the brute facts of experience. Becker's appeal to the nation to accept responsibility as a defender of Western civilization seemed to be firmly institutionalized in the factual existence of NATO and SEATO.

When Becker affirmed his relation to Western civilization, he did so because he had changed his view of the fundamental nature of American culture. The tradition of the Jeffersonian covenant, with its roots in the

157

Enlightenment and Puritanism, was built around the assumed contrast between America's natural simplicity and Europe's historical complexity. The drama of our history was the effort of the people to destroy the parasitical growth of historical complexity on the body politic. But Becker, after 1939, had abandoned hope that institutional and traditional complexity was destined to disappear from the world. The core of American culture, he now declared, was the heritage of institutions and traditions which our European ancestors had brought with them from across the ocean. In 1941 Becker stated that Americans, like Europeans, would always be faced with the existence of powerful government and an economy of large power groups. Americans, he said, must face the existence of power. Since we shared with our European cousins our values and a common problem of reconciling those values with the permanent existence of institutional complexity and power relationships, there was no longer a philosophical justification for American isolation.

By 1945, the heritage of the Jeffersonian covenant as defended by Beard seemed irrevocably shattered. By 1945, the new approach of Becker, which joined the American nation to Western civilization, seemed firmly established. This, however, was not the case. The Jeffersonian covenant remained very much alive; it found expression in the writing of many American historians. And the historian who has worked most diligently and persuasively to breathe life into this faltering tradition is Daniel Boorstin. Like so many of his predecessors, Professor Boorstin came to history from another background; he came to history from law because he accepted the responsibility of defending the American political tradition of national uniqueness.

But Boorstin, in order to defend the tradition, had to abandon the indefensible position of Charles Beard. There was no longer room for any rational hope that the major foundations of modern society would disappear. Boorstin's strategy must be directed toward a denial of that gap between the Jeffersonian ideal and the modern social reality with which Turner, Beard, Becker, and Parrington had been so concerned.

Daniel Boorstin reached intellectual maturity at Harvard during the Great Depression. He developed a strong commitment to major social and economic reform as a necessary policy to end the disintegration of the American economy, which he related to the irresponsible leadership of the American business community. He was also greatly concerned with the existence of Nazism in Germany and the manner in which many of its tenets, especially anti-Semitism, found parallel expression in the United States. He argued that there was a direct relationship between the immoral business leaders and the rise of anti-Semitism in America during the 1930's: "When the reactionaries say they are attacking the Jews, they are really attacking progress and defending reaction. . . . Equality under the law has been the principle of Americanism. But this idea has never been completely put into effect; powerful and ambitious men, entrenched privilege have opposed it. . . . Today, as never before in our country, greed and power are fiercely attacking this American principle in order to 'divide and rule.' " [1]

But the young Daniel Boorstin, on the eve of World War II, like Charles Beard in 1914, was sure of "the final victory of democracy and progress against . . . reaction." [2] And, like Beard, he was prepared to use his skills as a scholar to speed progress. He too saw the selfish reactionaries entrenched in power because they were protected in their irresponsible use of property by the American courts. But where Beard, the political scientist, saw the Constitution as the great obstacle to democratic reform, Boorstin, the lawyer and legal historian, found the major enemy of democratic reform in the American common-law tradition. To the extent that American lawyers were loyal to that tradition, Boorstin argued, they supported a reactionary *status quo* and blocked democratic progress.

In 1941, he published his first book, *The Mysterious Science of the Law*. It was an exposition of the philosophical assumptions on which Sir William Blackstone, during the eighteenth century, constructed his *Commentaries* on the laws of England. By this analysis of Blackstone, Boorstin planned to demonstrate to American lawyers the source of their law in eighteenth-century England.

Charles Beard, in his *An Economic Interpretation of the Constitution* in 1913, had analyzed the historical context in which the Constitution had been written in order to dispel the myth of the nonpartisan objectivity of its framers. The founding fathers, Beard had declared, were men of selfish economic interest who had written their economic interest into this supposedly impartial document. Now in 1941, Boorstin was illuminating the historical context in which the American common law had its origins. He, too, was attempting to dispel the myth of the nonpartisan objectivity of its framer. Blackstone, Boorstin declared, was a man of selfish economic interest who had written his economic interest into this supposedly impartial tradition.

For Beard, the founding fathers were representatives of an aristocratic capitalist class; they were afraid of the people. They designed the Constitution to check the will of the people and to protect the property of their aristocratic class. To put the Constitution beyond the reach of the people, the framers surrounded it with the aura of infallibility. This document, they argued, expresses natural law, and men do not have the power to modify natural law; this is not a human creation subject to the whims of history; it is eternal and immutable. For Boorstin, Blackstone was a representative of an aristocratic capitalist class that was afraid of the people. His *Commentaries* were designed to check the will of the people and to protect the property of this aristocratic class. To put the common law beyond the reach of the people, Blackstone surrounded it with the aura of infallibility. This law, he argued, expresses natural law, and men do not have the power to modify natural law; this is not a human creation subject to the whims of history; it is eternal and immutable.

Boorstin in 1941 was echoing the appeal of Charles Beard in 1914, that his colleagues distinguish between myth and reality. Let us, he urged, see the basis of American law for what it is — an ideological rationalization of the property rights of an aristocratic and irresponsible capitalist class opposed to progress and democracy. Let us recognize that "Blackstone's work . . . was the product of a particular time and a particular place . . . written specifically for the squirearchy, merchants, and law students of eighteenth-century England. It had been written under the influence of the temporary assumptions and ways of thought of the author's own time." [3] A close examination of the *Commentaries,* Boorstin declared, will demonstrate that "Blackstone's statements were influenced not by the desire to discover what he did not know, but by the desire to prove what he already believed." [4]

Historians of Blackstone, Boorstin continued, have been misled by the Englishman's affirmation that he was going to base his views on the new natural science of Newton and Locke. But how, asked Boorstin, did Blackstone actually use the new science in building his legal theory? When Blackstone argued that human law must be based on a rational understanding of natural law, he immediately added that men must approach this task of comprehending natural law with great humility because man's rational capacity is extremely weak and feeble. How then, Boorstin asked, could Blackstone offer men any hope that they would ever be able to lift law above the shifting sands of human custom to establish it on the eternal and immutable rock of nature? But observe the cleverness of Blackstone's argument. God wants man to understand His law which He has placed in nature's principles. Therefore, He has caused human society to embody many of the principles of natural law. Knowing this, man can, therefore, supplement his inadequate faculty of abstract reason with his stronger capacity for learning through direct, concrete experience.

Blackstone, Boorstin declared, then postulated a contradictory theory of progress and primitivism which reinforced the Englishman's commitment to his *status quo*. Progress, according to Blackstone, was a law of nature. Human society would improve whether or not men acted. And progress, for Blackstone, was the movement out of the ephemeral conditions of human society back to the primitive perfection of natural law which existed before human societies developed. Man was not to build a better world. Rather he was to disestablish what he had created in error and pride during the dark ages. Through reason, through the study of history, through personal experience, men would search out the laws of nature and conform to them. The increasing conformity to natural rather than human laws would be progress; it would also be a return to primitive innocence. Blackstone next delivered his readers from uncertainty and doubt as to how they could attain harmony with natural law. Rejoice Englishmen — this was Blackstone's proclamation — our common experience tells us that we are already in harmony with natural law. God has been so benevolent that He has caused our society to be built on nature's principles. Our traditions are not the ephemeral customs of history but the eternal and immutable principles of God and nature. Englishmen have unknowingly been blessed by that progress which has established their laws on the basis of primitive virtue. If the principles of English laws seem too confused and disorderly to be the reflection of the rational structure of natural law, this is only more evidence of the beneficence of God. It is according to God's will that there should be aesthetically pleasing disorder and apparent contradictions in the natural customs of Englishmen. Beauty is not expressed by cold and abstract rational structure but in the warmth of gentle complexity. This is more evidence of the mysterious guiding hand of God to provide for man's happiness. Englishmen could relax with the sure knowledge that they lived in a timeless world where God had blended the real and the ideal.

The essence of this perfect legal structure for Blackstone, Boorstin concluded, was summarized in the rights of Englishmen to life, liberty, and property. These formed not a trinity but a hierarchy of values leading upwards to the most important, property. The Englishman's right to life was the right to be treated in a humane fashion. But surely, Blackstone argued, the law of nature is benevolent and since English laws expressed natural law, they too must be benevolent. The existing legal order of England then perfectly fulfilled man's right to his life. The same thing could be said about the Englishman's right to liberty. All Englishmen have the right to free choice; inevitably, they would choose to live by natural law. And since English law embodied natural principle, then Englishmen freely chose to support the existing legal structure; Englishmen were free when they obeyed the law. But, for Blackstone, property, unlike life and liberty, was not subordinate to the law of society. The individual had an absolute right to property because it was the fundamental law of nature. God intended man to hold property because it was the orderly structure of property relations that made a peaceful society possible. It is only when a man is a property owner that he can responsibly exercise his rights to liberty. It is imperative then to support the existing legal structure because it has as its ultimate responsibility the protection of the natural law of property rights. Social peace would be destroyed if property rights were tampered with and property rights would be violated if the legal system were disturbed.

Here then, Boorstin declared, is the way in which Blackstone enlisted the new prestige of natural law in the eighteenth century to support the existing social and political and, above all, economic structure of England. And this, wrote Boorstin, is the foundation of the American legal tradition. We have accepted it as a neutral philosophy but it is clearly a system designed to protect the English property-owning aristocracy of the eighteenth century.

Boorstin's conclusion in 1941 was like that of Beard in 1914. He too had demonstrated that the philosophical assumptions and value system that served as the foundation for a major element of the existing order were in conflict with the assumptions and values of democracy. As Beard in 1914 had asked American intellectuals to choose either democracy and progress and the American way or property and reaction and foreign ideology, so now, on the eve of World War II, Boorstin posed the same choice to his generation.

Beard's faith in progress was seriously damaged during World War I; Daniel Boorstin's faith in a progress that would end the power of reactionary business interests disappeared during World War II. Boorstin was a member of a lost generation because he had made the self-conscious awareness of an ideological commitment the essence of being a thinking man. He had written on the last page of his study on Blackstone: "Reason must be used to show man the consequences of his system of values and to persuade others to accept that system. But man must know his values. . . . The all-important factor in this process of reason, then, is what one has a mind to do. If man is to be self-conscious, to know the limits and understand the purposes of his critical faculty, he must therefore be aware that his reason is serving a preconceived and desired purpose. Only in this way can man be sure he has given his reason a function which justifies its use. Only in this way can the student of institutions, instead of resting in a specious sense of freedom, be certain that his reasoning about society will subserve some moral end." [5] And without a faith in progress, Boorstin no longer had a moral end to support. If Boorstin no longer believed in an inevitable revolution that was to liberate the people from the business interests, what values could he find to provide the foundation on which to rebuild his intellectual life?

Daniel Boorstin's next book, *The Lost World of Thomas Jefferson*, appeared in 1948. Its title is a symbolic key to an understanding of Daniel Boorstin's philosophy of history. The whole tenor of the book is that of discovery — a wonderful, enthusiastic, fresh sense of discovery which Boorstin passionately wanted to share with literate America because he had found in Jefferson a position which made unnecessary the need for ideological commitment. Jefferson's views, as Boorstin interpreted them in the tradition of Parrington, were not ultimately related to values but were built on his experience with the facts of nature. Boorstin, in 1941, believed that he was caught up in a world of ideological commitment and conflict. Now he discovered that unlike Europeans and other human beings, Americans lived outside of culture in harmony with nature.

Boorstin began his analysis of the Jeffersonian outlook by defining the American environment in terms as simple and innocent as those of Bancroft in 1830: "When the intellectually and spiritually mature man of Europe first settled in America, he was forced to relive the childhood of the race. . . . The institutional scene in which American man has developed has lacked that accumulation from intervening stages which has been so dominant a feature of the European landscape." [6]

Jefferson recognized, Boorstin wrote, that a revolution had occurred which had separated Americans from European civilization; Americans had stepped out of European history into a state of nature. This new American civilization was without a revolutionary ideology because, as Jefferson had seen, Americans now found the principles of their way of life in nature and not in ideology. Europeans, living in a historical society, were forced to speculate about the nature of reality and were forced to become metaphysicians. Americans were practical and pragmatic. The European affirmed and the Jeffersonian denounced abstract reason as the means of achieving truth and ascertaining God's purposes.

One is struck at this point by Boorstin's failure to make any correlation between his earlier study of Blackstone and his analysis of Jefferson. In 1941, he had been certain that Blackstone's *Commentaries* had become an important part of the American imagination; he had seen the flow of English culture into the English colonies and into the American nation which had emerged from those colonies. Now he seemed equally certain that in 1800 American culture was predominantly a response to nature.

But even more interesting is the way in which he ignored the possible parallels between Blackstone's theory of reality and the Jeffersonian outlook on reality. Earlier, Boorstin had presented an extended argument to demonstrate that Blackstone theorized that Englishmen in the eighteenth century were living in harmony with nature's laws, but he did not now suggest that the Jeffersonian imagination might be related to this English tradition. Although it is true that Blackstone's emphasis was on the embodiment of natural principle in the details of English law while Jefferson's emphasis was on the embodiment of natural principle in the details of physical nature, nevertheless the parallels between the two positions as described by Boorstin are significant.

Boorstin had presented Blackstone as a conservative who proclaimed the perfection of God's natural creation as it was found in English laws. Now Boorstin presented Jefferson as a conservative who proclaimed the perfection of God's natural creation as it was found in the details of the American landscape: "The Creation seemed an end in itself. . . . Any temptation to confess unsureness about the purpose of life was smothered at the outset by confident affirmation of the aesthetic qualities of nature." [7]

According to Boorstin, Blackstone argued that the organic relationship between the actual laws of England and the principles of natural law had created in England a perfect fusion of what is and what ought to be, between the ideal and the real. Now Boorstin treated Jefferson in the same terms: "By admiring the universe as the complete and perfected work of divine artifice, by idealizing process and activity as themselves the end of life, the Jeffersonian was insisting that the values by which the universe was to be assessed were somehow implicit in nature. All facts were endowed with an ambiguous quality: they became normative as well as descriptive." [8]

In following Blackstone's argument to its final conclusion Boorstin had discovered that the Englishman was arguing that the highest spiritual purpose of man was the exercise of his faculties in the material world to the end of accumulating property. Now Boorstin defined the attitude of Jefferson similarly, with the difference, however, that for Boorstin in 1948 this was an attitude uniquely American: ". . . in Jeffersonianism man's destiny was somehow to be realized on this earth and right here in America. . . . The opportunity which man had never been given to play his destined role was now offered in the New World — not to fulfill an abstract moral purpose, but to realize the possibilities in the creation." [9]

For Blackstone, as Boorstin summarized his views, the natural order was surrounded by mystery and man should come to it with an attitude of deep reverence, aware that mortal man could never understand all of God's work, but filled with the faith that all of this creation, no matter what its surface appearance, reflected God's goodness and was designed for the ultimate happiness of man. And now Boorstin wrote that it was the unique attitude of the Jeffersonians to approach the natural creation with awe and reverence, filled with faith that nature's disorder or incompleteness or even evil was only appearance and that all seeming imperfections were unified in the mystery of a nature beyond man's rational comprehension: "The Jeffersonian found special pleasure in showing how facts which at first glance seemed to obstruct life processes proved on profounder examination actually to serve those processes." [10] Thus, Boorstin wrote, Jefferson could be confident that swamps, poisonous snakes, dread diseases like yellow fever, all fitted into the goodness of God's natural creation: "Although it might be beyond the philosopher's power to see the whole design, he was nonetheless sure that there had been no errata in the Book of Creation." [11]

This amazing parallel between the views of Blackstone and those of Jefferson continued to be developed by Boorstin but without an explicit recognition of that parallel. Blackstone, Boorstin had written, warned men that their capacity for analytical reasoning was inadequate for an understanding of God's creation, but since natural law was embodied in English life, men could find the principles of nature through their everyday experiences. Now Boorstin stated that Jefferson asked Americans to give up the European faith in abstract reason to learn about nature through experience. For Jefferson, "The philosopher's only hope was to flee from the weakness . . . of his brain, to the pure data of his senses. . . . 'Abstraction,' which was the prime occupation and the essential sin of metaphysics, was the greatest menace to all true philosophy. . . . the true philosopher would try to describe the particular facts of creation in all their complexity. . . . The lessons of philosophy were hardly to be distinguished from the fruits of experience." [12] As Blackstone found the laws of nature by examining the complex details of English legal practice, so Jefferson found the laws of nature by examining the complex details of American nature. And, like Blackstone, Jefferson refused to trust even individual experience; like Blackstone, he believed that "Since no one by himself could aspire to a serene knowledge of the whole truth, all men had been drawn into an active, exploratory and cooperative attitude." [13]

Boorstin had emphasized the way in which Blackstone had come to define individual freedom as the freedom to work within the natural order given to man by God. For Blackstone, political responsibility was to keep society in harmony with nature. Now Boorstin rediscovered this political approach in the writings of Thomas Jefferson. But he implied that Jefferson's views were unique because they grew from a confrontation with nature and that Europeans, living with history, could not imagine a natural harmony. What Jefferson asked of his political theory, Boorstin wrote, "was no blueprint for society, but a way of discovering the plan implicit in nature. . . . Political science, like all philosophy, was merely prophylactic; its aim was not the good society, but a healthy society. . . . For the Jeffersonian, God's government did not need to be imposed on nature since it was actually revealed there. Now it seemed that man's role was to realize all natural potentialities, rather than to shape or restrain them." [14]

Finally, Boorstin described the inability of the Jeffersonian to define clearly the society or community and, therefore, the responsibility of the individual to this nebulous group: "The Jeffersonian natural 'rights' philosophy was thus a declaration of inability or unwillingness to give positive form to the concept of community, or to face the need for defining explicitly the moral ends to be served by government. . . . His 'natural rights' theory of government left all men naturally free from duties to their neighbors: no claims could be validated except by the Creator's plan, and the Creator seemed to have made no duties but only rights." [15] Again Boorstin was implicitly contrasting American uniqueness and separation from the European imagination which, he asserted, did focus on the dutiful relationship of the individual to a well-defined community. But Boorstin had argued in his analysis of Blackstone that the Englishman had made the right of the individual to private property beyond community control. And Blackstone had definitely subordinated humanity to this individual right which transcended society. Like Jefferson, Blackstone had made the right to property absolute.

Ignoring the parallels between the philosophies of nature held by Blackstone and Jefferson, Boorstin made a sharp distinction between the European Blackstone, who had developed a legal philosophy to rationalize the interests of an economic class, and the American Jefferson, who had developed a natural philosophy which expressed the physical conditions of the American frontier. Boorstin insisted that Blackstone's philosophy was an expression of historical circumstances but that Jefferson's philosophy was an adaptation to nature; that Blackstone's philosophy was built upon human interests and values — it was an ideology — but that Jefferson's philosophy was not an ideology because it brought human interests and values into harmony with nature; that Blackstone might pretend that English law was timeless and eternal because it was a reflection of nature but it was only in America that such a timeless and eternal state of nature was available to European man.

Boorstin was openly nostalgic in his admiration for this lost world of Thomas Jefferson. But, in 1948, he believed that Jefferson's world had slipped beyond the grasp of twentieth-century Americans. He could not escape his ideological dilemma by retreating to this Eden where men had looked to nature for guidance. Sadly, he wrote: "Just as America will never again be the same kind of wilderness that it was in Jefferson's day, it is surely not in our power to live any more within the Jeffersonian world of ideas." [16] The urban-industrial revolution of the nineteenth century had separated Americans from physical nature and, therefore, from the Jeffersonian philosophy. But Boorstin was clearly distressed by this change; clearly, he despised the world of ideology: "The urban Leviathan — the railroad, the factory, and the encompassing city life — seemed to suggest that man somehow could actually build his own social universe. . . . One hundred years after Jefferson, man had arrogated to himself the energy, craftmanship and power of his Creator. When the success of the Jeffersonian struggle for mastery was thus realized then surely the check which saved the Jeffersonian from arrogance and dogma would be removed. When man should conceive himself his own Creator, the full danger of . . . 'the will to power through understanding of nature' would be laid bare." [17]

Boorstin had rediscovered the Jeffersonian covenant only to be aware that the American people had moved away from it as the physical frontier disappeared. They had become like Europeans, living in historical society; they had lost the harmony of nature. But was it really true that the American people had ceased to live with the Jeffersonian covenant? Obviously, institutional complexity had increased during the nineteenth century. But the presence of institutions did not make the difference between a Jeffersonian society and a European one. Boorstin had found that there were institutions in Jefferson's America but, in contrast to the European viewpoint that institutions were the source of values, "Institutions, from the Jeffersonian point of view, were not the skeleton but the instruments of society; they were therefore conceived, not as growing imperceptibly and by accretion, but as being consciously and purposely shaped, to be repaired or discarded when they had lost their immediate utility. Not institutions, but nature itself was the receptacle and vehicle of values." [18]

Now if it were true that in America the majority of the people had continued to work within this philosophy during the nineteenth century, then the new institutional complexity had not necessarily come between the people and nature. Perhaps Americans had merely increased the number of their tools of adjustment to nature. Perhaps the American people had not arrogated "the energy, craftmanship and power" of the Creator. It was possible then that it was not the urban-industrial frontier which had brought Americans to ideological difficulties in the middle of the twentieth century. Perhaps it was only American intellectuals, overly influenced by European ideas, who had come to imagine that they were part of the European historical environment, who had come to share in the dilemmas of European culture, who were lost without bearings in the chartless seas of European ideology. For some reason, they did not know that American society was built on the eternal and immutable rock of natural principles. In 1953, he expressed these possibilities as certainties in his book *The Genius of American Politics*.

At the conclusion of *The Lost World of Thomas Jefferson*, Boorstin had not compared the pragmatic and mystical conservatism of Jefferson to that of Blackstone but rather to the ancient Hebrew prophets, like Jeremiah, who "Without elaborate theology, or metaphysics . . . dealt with the concrete, the personal, and the here-and-now; he sought less to fathom the thoughts of God, than to find His commandments of men. He was less interested in major premises than in conclusions. His aim was not the intellectual knowledge of God, but the practical imitation of Him." [19] Jeremiah, not Blackstone, became the self-conscious model for Daniel Boorstin to follow as he called in *The Genius of American Politics* for the American people to follow him back to the Jeffersonian covenant. But for those who had read Boorstin's analysis of Blackstone, it would be difficult not to find significant parallels between Daniel Boorstin as the political philosopher of American conservatism and William Blackstone, political philosopher of English conservatism.

Like Blackstone, Boorstin proclaimed that his people's perfection was not the result of conscious choice but was the gift of divine providence: ". . . the genius of American democracy comes not from any special virtue of the American people but from the unprecedented opportunities of this continent and from a peculiar and unrepeatable combination of historical circumstance." [20] He too affirmed that his people's only freedom was to conserve God's gift. "Our history has fitted us . . . to understand the meaning of conservatism." [21] In the manner of the Englishman, Boorstin argued that men discovered God in the details of life, not in abstract reason. "The unspoiled grandeur of America helped men believe that here the Giver of values spoke to man more directly — in the language of experience rather than in that of books or monuments." [22] As Blackstone had announced that eighteenth-century philosophers had discovered that nature's principles were already embodied in England's historical culture, so Boorstin also announced that America's eighteenth-century "Revolution itself . . . had been a kind of affirmation of faith in ancient British institutions." [23]

Blackstone had sadly contemplated the continental Europeans whose historical traditions and institutions did not embody natural law and had pitied their feeble attempts to copy what God had given England. Now Boorstin explained the modern Europeans' predilection for political theory as their vain attempt to imitate God's creation in America. And he explained the prevalence of theology in Europe as still another ideological attempt to escape the disharmony of history. Like Blackstone, he warned his people not to let their imaginations wander along the lines of European political theory or theology. Let us always remember, he admonished, that God has given us a good society and we find our political and spiritual values within its structure. This is why American "religions are instrumental. They commend themselves to us for the services they perform more than the truths which they affirm." [24]

If Americans were a people who had stepped out of history to live in harmony with nature, if the people had kept to the Jeffersonian covenant even with the apparent growth of institutional complexity, if Americans were indeed a blessed people who had escaped from the tragedy of the European past, what did Boorstin find wrong with America?

Bancroft, Turner, and Beard had seen the sanctity of the American people threatened by an artificial business aristocracy which made it possible for English culture to infiltrate the nation. Down to 1940, Beard had kept alive the hope that ultimately the institutionalized structure of American society would be swept away and the free individual of the Jeffersonian covenant restored to his harmony with nature. But for Boorstin, Beard was wrong in believing that Jefferson's America was subverted by the development of an artificial institutional complexity in economics and politics which provided power to a parasitical aristocracy to control the community. Like Blackstone, Boorstin found that the institutional complexity of his nation was itself natural.

The great impending tragedy that Beard had seen in 1940 was, therefore, a figment of his imagination. This, Boorstin declared, was the basic problem in América at mid-century. There was an artificial elite, the intellectuals, who had been corrupted by European culture. Looking at America with the perspective of European ideology, they had imagined that Americans were trapped by institutions of the European type, institutions which incorporated the irrationalities of a tragic history, and they had been led to adopt the European heresy that men must transcend their social environment to create a good society.

Now Daniel Boorstin appeared in all his theological strength as the Jeffersonian Jeremiah. Loudly and clearly, he appealed to American intellectuals that they repent their errors which had made them critics of the American *status quo*. Let the scales drop from your eyes, he begged, and see how the ideal and the real are organically one in America. Understand how, as idealists, it is your responsibility to defend everything as it now exists. Realize that the first Americans who began to lead you astray were philosophers like "Josiah Royce, Henry George, and Herbert Croly, who, almost without exception, wanted a larger role for the state, a role more like what was familiar in nineteenth-century Europe, where political parties embodied political philosophies." [25] Know that American historians like Beard have misunderstood American history because "They miss the essential point that the whole American experience has been utopian." [26] The essence of this utopian experience for Boorstin was its foundation in a state of nature which incorporated English traditions and which was leading to a progressive future: "Because we in America, more than other peoples of modern history, seemed situated to start life anew, we have been better able to see how much man inevitably retains of his past. For here, even with an unexampled opportunity for cultural rebirth, the American has remained plainly the inheritor of European laws, culture and institutions. . . . It is not surprising that we have no enthusiasm for plans to make society over. We have actually made a new society without a plan. . . . From this point of view, the proper role of the citizen and the statesman here is one of conservatism and reform rather than of invention. He is free to occupy himself with the means of improving his society; for there is relatively little disagreement on ends. Turner summed it up when he said: 'The problem of the United States is not to create democracy, but to conserve democratic institutions and ideals.'" [27]

We have no political theory and no political institutions to export, wrote Boorstin, because our theories and our institutions have developed organically from our nation's origin in a state of nature. "The European concept of a political community is of a group oriented toward fulfilling an explicit philosophy; political life there is the world of ends and absolutes." [28] In the United States, however, political life is the fulfillment of natural principles; political life here is one of means and pragmatic principles. Americans then "must refuse to become crusaders for liberalism, in order to remain liberals. . . . We must refuse to become crusaders for conservatism, in order to conserve the institutions and the genius which have made America great." [29]

Daniel Boorstin had made his impassioned plea to American intellectuals to give up the unreality of European ideology and return to the natural harmony of the American experience. But to redeem the intellectuals, to lead them back to the covenant, would require an objective demonstration of the affirmations of *The Genius of American Politics*. Boorstin had the responsibility of writing a great synthesis of national history comparable to that of Charles Beard to prove that Beard was wrong and that the natural harmony of America had remained constant from the seventeenth century until the present. He would have to demonstrate in historical detail that Europeans had stepped out of history into America and that this utopian experience was still the basis of American life in the second half of the twentieth century.

With *The Americans: The Colonial Experience,* published in 1958, Daniel Boorstin laid the foundationstone for this epic synthesis. One is not surprised by Boorstin's opening statement: "America began as a sobering experience. The colonies were a disproving ground for utopias. In the following chapters we will illustrate how dreams made in Europe . . . were dissipated or transformed by the American reality. A new civilization was being born less out of plans and purposes than out of the unsettlement which the New World brought to the ways of the Old." [30]

Bancroft, Turner, and Beard had all argued that when European man had stepped out of history into nature, the European had left his institutional and traditional life behind. Boorstin, however, had found the intellectual formula which proved to Americans that they could believe that they had a natural simplicity which cut them off from the complexity of European history but that this simplicity was one of vast institutional and traditional complexity. It was a formula which allowed Boorstin to continue to play the role of a Blackstone for his society.

Yes, Boorstin wrote, European man brought European traditions and institutions across the ocean and used them to build the foundations of a new society. But in Europe, man inherited institutions and traditions within the context of an established historical society and was, therefore, the prisoner of his inherited institutions and traditions. When European man crossed the Atlantic, he used his inherited institutions and traditions as the tools to adjust to physical nature and to build the new society. The American, therefore, controlled his institutions and traditions in a society designed to bring and keep men in harmony with nature. Social complexity in America was organically related to nature.

In this volume, Boorstin examined four English colonial experiments: the Puritan, the Quaker, the Virginian, and the Georgian. He found that the Puritans, the Virginians, and the Georgians abandoned European ideology and used their European institutions pragmatically to adjust to the unique environmental pressures they met in their different geographic areas. But the Quakers, he wrote, refused to become Americans: "One of the distinctive features of the Pennsylvania experiment was that American Quakers were subject to constant persuasion, surveillance, and scrutiny from afar. The powerful rulers of the London Yearly Meeting were remote from the perils, opportunities, and challenges of America; yet their influence was a check on what might have been the normal adaptation of Quaker doctrines to life in America. The Society of Friends had become a kind of international conspiracy for Peace and for primitive Christian perfection." [31]

Fortunately, for Boorstin, the Quakers were overwhelmed by the general development of American culture in the English colonies. And instead of Quaker idealism, the majority of Americans developed the philosophy of pragmatism. Here, Boorstin wrote, was "The most fertile novelty of the New World . . . its new concept of knowledge. . . . The time had come for the over-cultivated man of Europe to rediscover the earth on which he walked." [32] Americans gave up the tradition of learning for practical education; they did not want scholars but good citizens. Philosophy and theology, after all, were unnecessary when men had achieved the materialist utopia. "Was not the New World a living denial of the old sharp distinction between the world as it was and the world as it might be or ought to be?" [33]

By 1960, Daniel Boorstin appeared to have established a successful Jeremiad. He had minimized the moral dramas of Bancroft and Beard by denying the conflict between the people and an alien aristocracy. The only threat to the national covenant came from confused and misinformed intellectuals and they were to be educated into the truth that American complexity did not challenge the purity and simplicity of the community. The moral dramas of Bancroft and Beard existed only in the imaginations of these historians who had been overly influenced by European ideology.

But in 1962, Boorstin published *The Image* which seemed to deny much of the intellectual position he had constructed over the last decade. He appeared to have discovered a more fearful threat to American innocence than those which had haunted Bancroft, Turner, Becker, Parrington, and Beard. He found corruption within the "people."

His opening statement in this book captures all the puritanical disgust of Vernon Parrington's discovery that the American people had abandoned the Jeffersonian covenant in the early nineteenth century to follow the European idea of material progress: "In this book I describe the world of our making, how we have used our wealth, our literacy, our technology, and our progress, to create the thicket of unreality which stands between us and the facts of life. . . . We want and we believe these illusions because we suffer from extravagant expectations. We expect too much of the world." [34] For Boorstin, the metaphysical reality of American simplicity was being abandoned by the people, who were choosing to live with artificial complexity. "What ails us most is not what we have done with America, but what we have substituted for America. . . . We are haunted, not by reality, but by those images we have put in place of reality." [35]

The great responsibility for Boorstin, the Jeffersonian Jeremiah, was now to describe this artificiality, hoping that when the people became aware that they were living within an artificial society, they would choose to return to the reality of the Jeffersonian covenant.

But in exposing this unreal world, Boorstin, again like Parrington, was forced to reunite American with European history; he had to admit that something had happened in America since 1800 and that these occurrences were parallels of movements in Europe. The Jeffersonian ideal of permanence and stability had been destroyed by the "Democratic Revolutions of the eighteenth and nineteenth centuries and the Graphic Revolution of the nineteenth and twentieth centuries." [36] Boorstin, who had written rhapsodic praise for the American tradition of pragmatic and utilitarian education as late as 1958, now criticized the people for accepting a democratic philosophy of education that rejected fixed standards of values. "A stigma, the odium of an outdated priestly aristocracy, was put on anything that could not be made universally intelligible. Equalitarian America attached a new, disproportionate importance to the knowledge which all could get and to techniques which all could master." And "The whole American tradition of pragmatism . . . has expressed a consuming interest in the appearances of things." [37]

This shift away from absolute standards caused by the Democratic Revolution, he continued, led to the affirmation that each man was his own standard and this loss of contact with reality was reinforced by the Graphic Revolution which "has multiplied and vivified images." Mass production, the interchangeability of parts, the rise of advertising, the speed of transportation have reinforced the drift away from fixed, unchanging principles to a fabricated, false, artificial world of images. "We reversed traditional ways of thinking about the relation between images and ideals. Instead of thinking that an image was only a representation of an ideal, we came to see the ideal as a projection or generalization of an image. . . . We distrusted any standard of perfection toward which all people could strive." [38]

But what was that standard of perfection toward which Boorstin would have the American people strive? Following Blackstone, he had argued that man should endeavor to follow the natural laws one discovered by commonsense experience in society, that one could not discover first principles through the use of abstract reason, and that the ought and the is were organically unified in the current society. Like Blackstone, he had denied the possibility of standing outside the *status quo* and criticizing it.

But now Boorstin was standing outside his society and criticizing its forms. On what philosophical position could he take such a stand? Dogma and ideology, philosophy and theology, were European and had no place in the New World. Boorstin had argued in *The Genius of American Politics* that there was no way of describing the American way of life in theoretical terms and that there should be no possibility of an abstract definition of the nation. He had written: "When we penetrate the Holy of Holies of our national faith, we must not expect the glittering jewels and filigreed relics of a pagan temple. The story is told that when the Temple of Solomon in Jerusalem fell in 63 B.C. and Pompey invaded the Holy of Holies, he found to his astonishment that it was empty. This was, of course, a symbol of the absence of idolatry, which was the essential truth of Judaism. Perhaps the same surprise awaits the student of American culture. . . . Far from being disappointed, we should be inspired that in an era of idolatry . . . we have had the courage . . . to keep the sanctum empty." [39]

If then the sanctuary of American ideals was empty, what standards should the Americans use to distinguish between the image and the ideal? When Daniel Boorstin cast doubt on popular culture, when he questioned the values of the people, he removed himself from the tradition of the American Jeremiad, which had the purpose of saving the people from the temptation of foreign ideology. Boorstin blamed this new corruption on American advertising, on magazines like the *Reader's Digest*.[40] How could these be identified with alien ideology? Boorstin has sundered the organic unity of the is and the ought, the real and the ideal, that had marked America's philosophy of history. He has placed the moral drama of a threat to the Jeffersonian covenant within the community itself. And he provides little assurance that the people will cease to wander along strange paths away from the ark of the covenant of arcadian simplicity.

10 THE END OF THE COVENANT AND THE BEGINNING OF AMERICAN HISTORY

Even while Daniel Boorstin attempts to preserve the Jeffersonian covenant by weaving it into the existing traditions and institutions of our culture, we recognize that our nation's traditional vision of its historical existence has reached an ideological impasse. The Puritans of the seventeenth century reacted to the disintegration of the medieval community by reaching out for a covenant with God that would provide them with earthly security. They came to believe that the collapse of the medieval social structure did not signify disaster for Europe but rather that it could be defined as progress. God, they argued, did not want man to live within a framework of historical institutions and traditions. God wanted every man to live simply and purely as an unfettered individual. In their covenant with God, the Puritans promised, therefore, that they would build no new institutions or traditions, they would create no new social complexity once God had delivered them from the oppression of the medieval past.

Our historians from Bancroft to Beard asserted that the reality of the American experience was this Puritan covenant translated into the material form of the Jeffersonian republic. Americans, they wrote, live not as members of a historical community with its inevitable structure of institutions and traditions, but as the children of nature who are given earthly definition by the virgin land that had redeemed their ancestors when they stepped out of the shifting sands of European history. Our historians, until World War II, proclaimed that Europe was history and America was nature because the Old World had institutions and traditions

176

and the New World had none. Now, however, as our commonsense experience forces us to admit that we live in a highly complex urban-industrial society, historians like Daniel Boorstin who still defend the idea of a national covenant must persuade us that while this complexity of institutions and traditions exists, it does not signify that we have broken the oath of our Puritan ancestors not to create a new historical culture to replace the fast vanishing medieval community. But what indeed is left of the Puritan covenant when we have to argue that current social structure, with its rich variety of institutions and traditions, does not violate its sanctity?

With this admission of complexity, it may be possible that in the future more American historians will look back to Carl Becker's break from the Jeffersonian covenant to find a way to relate American history both to its roots in the past and to its own fascinating record of development. It is possible that American historians will increasingly come to understand Becker's final conclusion that, unless Americans admit they are connected to previous historical traditions and previous historical institutions, they cannot visualize a creative future. For, if Americans have no past, they have no future; they are doomed by the burden of innocence to repeat endlessly that only in America is there no historical drama; they are fated to deny the reality of their existence.

What Becker finally saw was that, in the name of individualism, the frontier tradition denied moral responsibility to the individual by taking away the possibility of choice and creativity. He learned that the individualism of that tradition was completely negative. The individual was freed from the medieval past to live in harmony with nature. The individual did not create a good society. America, as nature, was merely the absence of the European past. And for Americans, there was not even the creativity of destroying the medieval heritage. This was done for them by the impersonal force first of the physical frontier and then the industrial frontier. Bancroft, Beard, and Boorstin are all in agreement that creative social action by the individual involves power and, for them, power necessarily corrupts. To preserve their innocence, Americans have the responsibility not to act. And, as Becker pointed out, the puritanical decree against social activity logically leads to a puritanical decree against creative thinking. The historians of the frontier tradition have all objected to analytical philosophy, analytical theology, and analytical political theory because they have postulated the organic unity of the real and the ideal, which precludes the necessity of analytical thought in the promised land. When all the fundamental problems of human existence are resolved, it follows logi-cally that men will content themselves with a pragmatic appreciation of perfection.

As Carl Becker asked in 1941, so again we must ask: Can Americans afford the romantic illusion of a completed destiny in the twentieth century? Are Americans to be such prisoners of ideology that they are cut off from creative action to meet the massive problems of a revolutionary society at home and abroad?

Notes

NOTES

Chapter 1. Flight from Feudalism

[1] Quoted in Carl Becker, *The Heavenly City of the Eighteenth Century Philosophers* (New Haven: Yale University Press, 1932), p. 95.

[2] Quoted in Durand Echeverria, *Mirage in the West* (Princeton, N.J.: Princeton University Press, 1957), p. 31.

[3] Quoted in *ibid.*, pp. 32–33.

[4] Quoted in *ibid.*, p. 73.

[5] Quoted in *ibid.*, p. 69.

[6] Quoted in Daniel Boorstin, *The Lost World of Thomas Jefferson* (New York: Holt, 1948), p. 228.

[7] Quoted in *ibid.*, p. 291.

[8] Quoted in *ibid.*, p. 231.

Chapter 2. George Bancroft

[1] Russel B. Nye, *George Bancroft: Brahmin Rebel* (New York: Knopf, 1944).

[2] George Bancroft, *History of the United States*, Volume III (Boston: Little, Brown, 1840), p. 399.

[3] George Bancroft, *Literary and Historical Miscellanies* (New York, 1855), pp. 489, 490.

[4] *Ibid.*, p. 482.

[5] *Ibid.*, pp. 483, 488.

[6] *Ibid.*, p. 409.

[7] *Ibid.*, p. 415.

[8] *Ibid.*, pp. 423, 425.

[9] Bancroft, *History of the United States*, II (1837), 453, 454.

[10] *Ibid.*, I (1834), 231, 232.

[11] *Ibid.*, p. 265.

[12] *Ibid.*, pp. 402, 403.

[13] *Ibid.*, II, 451.

[14] *Ibid.*, IV, 276–277.

[15] *Ibid.*, V (1852), 4.

[16] *Ibid.*, I, 231, 232.

[17] *Ibid.*, IX (1866), 260.

[18] *Ibid.*, VII (1858), 394.

[19] *Ibid.*, VIII (1860), 462, 463

[20] *Ibid.*, VIII, 383.

[21] *Ibid.*, IX, 257; II, 145; VIII, 473

[22] *Ibid.*, VIII, 474.

[23] *Ibid.*, IV, 12.

[24] Bancroft, *Literary and Historical Miscellanies*, pp. 449, 450.

[25] *Ibid.*, pp. 462, 463.

[26] *Ibid.*, p. 465

[27] Bancroft, *Memorial Address on the Life and Character of Abraham Lincoln* (Washington, D.C.: Government Printing Office, 1866), pp. 16, 17.

[28] *Ibid.*, pp. 34, 35.

[29] *Ibid.*, p. 51.

Chapter 3. Frederick Jackson Turner

[1] Frederick Jackson Turner, "The Significance of the Frontier in American History," reprinted in *The Frontier in American History* (New York: 1920; republished, New York: Holt, Rinehart, and Winston, 1962), p. 1. For biographical and bibliographical information on Turner, see Harvey Wish, *The American Historian* (New York: Oxford University Press, 1960) and Lee Benson, *Turner and Beard: American Historical Writing Reconsidered* (Glencoe, Ill.: Free Press, 1960).

[2] Turner, *The Frontier in American History*, p. 11.

[3] Quoted in Henry Nash Smith, *Virgin Land* (Cambridge, Mass.: Harvard University Press, 1950), p. 253.

[4] Turner, *The Frontier in American History*, p. 267.

[5] Quoted in Smith, *Virgin Land*, p. 296n12.

[6] Turner, *The Frontier in American History*, p. 3.

[7] Turner, *The Early Writings of Frederick Jackson Turner* (Madison: University of Wisconsin Press, 1938), pp. 49–50, 52.

[8] *Ibid.*, pp. 43, 44.

[9] *Ibid.*, p. 107.

[10] Turner, *The Frontier in American History*, p. 18.

[11] Turner, *The Early Writings*, p. 250.

[12] *Ibid.*, p. 251.

[13] Turner, *The Rise of the New West* (New York: Harper, 1906), pp. 331–332.

[14] *Ibid.*, p. 332.

[15] Turner, *The United States, 1830–1850* (New York: Holt, 1935), p. 77.

[16] *Ibid.*, p. 30.

[17] *Ibid.*, p. 351.

[18] Turner, *The Frontier in American History*, pp. 303–304.

[19] Turner, *The United States, 1830–1850*, pp. 86, 89.

[20] Turner, *The Frontier in American History*, p. 261.

[21] *Ibid.*

[22] *Ibid.*, pp. 238, 239, 240.

[23] *Ibid.*, pp. 356, 357–358.

[24] *Ibid.*, p. 286.

[25] *Ibid.*, p. 203.

[26] *Ibid.*, p. 244.

[27] *Ibid.*, p. 311.

[28] *Ibid.*, p. 317.

Chapter 4. Charles A. Beard

[1] Charles A. Beard, *The Industrial Revolution* (London: S. Sonnenschein, 1901), pp. 1, 23. For biographical and bibliographical material on Beard, see Wish, *The American Historian*, and Benson, *Turner and Beard*.

[2] *Ibid.*, p. 79.

[3] *Ibid.*, p. 53.

[4] *Ibid.*, p. 79.

[5] James Harvey Robinson and Charles A. Beard, *The Development of Modern Europe* (2 vols.; Boston: Ginn, 1907), I, 167.

[6] *Ibid.*, II, 405.

[7] Beard, "Politics," *Lectures on Science, Philosophy and Art* (New York: Columbia University, 1908), pp. 9–10.

[8] *Ibid.*, p. 21.

[9] *Ibid.*, pp. 21–22.

[10] *Ibid.*, p. 30.

[11] Beard, *American Government and Politics* (New York: Macmillan, 1910), pp. 1–2.

[12] *Ibid.*, p. 35.

[13] *Ibid.*, pp. 46–47.

[14] Beard, *The Supreme Court and the Constitution* (New York: Macmillan, 1912), pp. 84–85.

[15] *Ibid.*, p. 88.

[16] Beard, book review, *American Historical Review*, XVIII (January 1913), 379.

[17] Beard, *Contemporary American History* (New York: Macmillan, 1914), p. 305.

[18] *Ibid.*, p. 315.

[19] Beard, *An Economic Interpretation of the Constitution of the United States* (New York: Macmillan, 1913), p. 63.

[20] *Ibid.*, p. 154.

[21] Beard, "Jefferson and the New Freedom," *New Republic*, I (November 14, 1914), 19.

[22] Beard, *The Economic Origins of Jeffersonian Democracy* (New York: Macmillan, 1915).

[23] Beard, *American Citizenship* (New York: Macmillan, 1914), p. 6, and *American City Government* (New York: Century, 1912).

[24] Beard, "Historical Woman Suffrage," *New Republic*, IV (October 9, 1915), 3.

[25] Frederic A. Ogg and Charles A. Beard, *National Governments and the World War* (New York: Macmillan, 1919), pp. 1, 2.

[26] *Ibid.*, pp. 562, 570.

[27] Charles A. Beard and William C. Bagley, *The History of the American People* (New York: Macmillan, 1919), p. 102.

[28] *Ibid.*, p. 223.

[29] *Ibid.*, p. 312.

[30] Beard, *Cross Currents in Europe To-day* (Boston: Marshall Jones, 1922), p. 2.

[31] *Ibid.*, p. 138.

[32] Beard, *The Economic Basis of Politics* (New York: Knopf, 1922).

Chapter 5. Carl Becker

[1] Letter to Turner quoted in Burleigh T. Wilkins, *Carl Becker: A Biographical Study in American Intellectual History* (Cambridge, Mass.: MIT Press, 1961), p. 32. Mr. Wilkins' book provides biographical and bibliographical material on Becker.

[2] Becker, *The History of Political Parties in the Province of New York, 1760–1776,* Bulletin of the University of Wisconsin, no. 286 (Madison, 1909), p. 5.

[3] Becker, "Detachment and the Writing of History," *Atlantic Monthly*, CVI (October 1910), 525.

[4] Becker, *Everyman His Own Historian* (New York: Crofts, 1935), p. 19.

[5] Becker, "Some Aspects of the Influence of Social Problems and Ideas upon

the Study and Writing of History," *American Journal of Sociology*, XVIII (March 1913), 675.

⁶ For his criticism of practical, democratic education, see his essay of 1917, "On Being a Professor," reprinted in *Detachment and the Writing of History: Essays and Letters of Carl L. Becker*, edited by Phil L. Snyder (Ithaca, N.Y.: Cornell University Press, 1958), pp. 91–113.

⁷ Review of L. Cecil Jane's *The Interpretation of History* in *Dial*, LIX (September 2, 1915), 148.

⁸ *Ibid.*

⁹ Becker, *Everyman His Own Historian*, p. 281.

¹⁰ Becker, "The Monroe Doctrine and the War," *Minnesota History Bulletin*, II (May 1917), 16–68.

¹¹ Becker, "German Attempts to Divide Belgium," *World Peace Foundation* (Boston), Vol. 1, No. 6 (August 1918), 308–309.

¹² War Information Series, Committee on Public Information, No. 21 (November 1918).

¹³ Becker, *The Eve of the Revolution* (New Haven: Yale University Press, 1918), p. 256.

¹⁴ Becker, *Our Great Experiment in Democracy* (New York: Harper, 1920), p. 6.

¹⁵ *Ibid.*, pp. 317, 322.

¹⁶ Quoted in Wilkins, *Carl Becker*, pp. 132, 133.

¹⁷ Becker, *Detachment and the Writing of History*, p. 33.

¹⁸ *Ibid.*, p. 185.

¹⁹ Becker, *The Declaration of Independence* (New York: Harcourt, Brace, 1922), p. 39.

²⁰ *Ibid.*, p. 218.

²¹ *Ibid.*, pp. 278–279.

²² Becker, *Detachment and the Writing of History*, p. 45.

²³ *Ibid.*, pp. 62–63.

²⁴ Becker, *Everyman His Own Historian*, p. 177.

²⁵ *Ibid.*, p. 185.

²⁶ *Ibid.*, p. 187.

²⁷ Becker, *The Heavenly City of the Eighteenth Century Philosophers*, p. 7.

²⁸ *Ibid.*, p. 16.

Chapter 6. Vernon Louis Parrington

¹ Vernon Louis Parrington, *Main Currents in American Thought*, Volume I: *The Colonial Mind* (New York: Harcourt, Brace, 1927), p. 11. See Wish, *The American Historian*, for biographical information.

² Parrington, *Main Currents in American Thought*, I, 50.

³ *Ibid.*, pp. 108, 110.

⁴ *Ibid.*, p. 120.

⁵ *Ibid.*, p. 168.

⁶ *Ibid.*, p. 184.

⁷ *Ibid.*, p. 188.

⁸ *Ibid.*, pp. 193–194.

⁹ *Ibid.*, p. 197.

¹⁰ *Ibid.*, p. 351.

¹¹ *Ibid.*, p. 401.

¹² *Ibid.*, p. 402.

¹³ Parrington, *Main Currents in American Thought*, Volume II: *The Romantic Revolution in America* (New York: Harcourt, Brace, 1927), pp. ix–x.

¹⁴ *Ibid.*, p. 78.

¹⁵ *Ibid.*, p. 131.

[16] *Ibid.*, pp. 138–139.

[17] *Ibid.*, p. 137.

[18] *Ibid.*, p. 145.

[19] *Ibid.*, p. 153.

[20] *Ibid.*, p. 374.

[21] *Ibid.*, p. 389.

[22] *Ibid.*, pp. 405–406.

[23] *Ibid.*, p. 465.

[24] Parrington, *Main Currents in American Thought*, Volume III: *The Beginnings of Critical Realism in America* (New York: Harcourt, Brace, 1930), p. 4.

[25] *Ibid.*, p. 86.

[26] *Ibid.*, p. 100.

[27] *Ibid.*, pp. 81–82.

[28] *Ibid.*, p. 284.

[29] *Ibid.*, p. 191.

Chapter 7. Beard

[1] Charles and Mary Beard, *The Rise of American Civilization* (2 vols.; New York: Macmillan, 1927), I, 88.

[2] *Ibid.*, p. 118.

[3] *Ibid.*, pp. 256, 264.

[4] *Ibid.*, pp. 299–300.

[5] *Ibid.*, p. 328.

[6] *Ibid.*, pp. 514, 516–517, 534, 535.

[7] *Ibid.*, II, 53, 105.

[8] *Ibid.*, p. 198.

[9] *Ibid.*, pp. 397, 247.

[10] *Ibid.*, p. 399.

[11] *Ibid.*, pp. 568, 569, 589.

[12] *Ibid.*, p. 800.

[13] Charles and William Beard, *The American Leviathan* (New York: Macmillan, 1930), pp. vii, 3.

[14] Beard, ed., *America Faces the Future* (Boston: Houghton Mifflin, 1932), pp. 117–139.

[15] Beard with George H. E. Smith, *The Future Comes* (New York: Macmillan, 1933), pp. 161–164.

[16] Beard, "Rushlights in the Darkness," *Scribner's*, XC (December 1931), 578.

[17] J. B. Bury, *The Idea of Progress* (New York: Macmillan, 1932), pp. xxiii–xxiv.

[18] Beard, "Written History as an Act of Faith," *American Historical Review*, XXXIX (January 1934), 219.

[19] Beard with George H. E. Smith, *The Idea of National Interest* (New York: Macmillan, 1934), p. 87.

[20] *Ibid.*, p. 85.

[21] Beard with George H. E. Smith, *The Open Door at Home* (New York: Macmillan, 1934).

[22] Beard, "National Politics and War," *Scribner's*, 97 (February 1935), 65–70.

[23] Charles Beard with Mary Beard, *America in Midpassage* (New York: Macmillan, 1939), p. 767.

[24] *Ibid.*, pp. 947–948.

[25] Beard, *Giddy Minds and Foreign Quarrels* (New York: Macmillan, 1939) and *A Foreign Policy for America* (New York: Knopf, 1940).

[26] Beard with George H. E. Smith, *The Old Deal and the New* (New York: Macmillan, 1940), p. 174.

[27] *Ibid.*, p. 279.

[28] Beard, *President Roosevelt and the Coming of the War 1941* (New Haven: Yale University Press, 1948).

[29] Beard, *The Republic* (New York: Viking, 1943), p. 342.

[30] Beard, *The American Spirit* (New York: Macmillan, 1942), p. 164.

[31] *Ibid.*, p. 538.

[32] *Ibid.*, p. 594.

[33] *Ibid.*, pp. 652–653.

[34] *Ibid.*, p. 674.

Chapter 8. Becker

[1] Becker, *The Heavenly City*, p. 167.

[2] Becker, *Everyman His Own Historian*, pp. 89–90.

[3] *Ibid.*, p. 248.

[4] *Ibid.*, p. 253.

[5] Becker, *Modern History* (New York: Silver, Burdett, 1931), p. vi.

[6] Becker, *Detachment and the Writing of History*, p. 201.

[7] *Ibid.*, pp. 211–212.

[8] Becker, *Progress and Power* (Palo Alto, Calif.: Stanford University Press, 1936), p. 15.

[9] *Ibid.*, p. 51.

[10] *Ibid.*, p. 63.

[11] *Ibid.*, pp. 75, 77, 79.

[12] *Ibid.*, p. 80.

[13] *Ibid.*, p. 87.

[14] *Ibid.*, p. 94.

[15] *Ibid.*, p. 97.

[16] Becker, *New Liberties for Old* (New Haven: Yale University Press, 1941), p. 42.

[17] *Ibid.*, p. 43.

[18] *Ibid.*, p. 93.

[19] *Ibid.*, p. 94.

[20] *Ibid.*, pp. 118–119.

[21] *Ibid.*, p. 134.

[22] *Ibid.*, pp. 140–141.

[23] *Ibid.*, p. 149.

[24] *Ibid.*, p. 168.

[25] Becker, *Modern Democracy* (New Haven: Yale University Press, 1941).

[26] Becker, *Detachment and the Writing of History*, p. 231.

[27] Becker, *How New Will the Better World Be?* (New York: Knopf, 1944), frontispiece.

[28] *Ibid.*, p. 246.

Chapter 9. Daniel Boorstin

[1] Daniel Boorstin, George Mayberry, John Rackliffe, *Anti-Semitism, A Threat to Democracy* (Boston, 1939), pp. 29, 30.

[2] *Ibid.*, p. 32.

[3] Boorstin, *The Mysterious Science of the Law* (Cambridge, Mass.: Harvard University Press, 1941), pp. 4–5.

[4] *Ibid.*, p. 6.

[5] *Ibid.*, p. 191.

[6] Boorstin, *The Lost World of Thomas Jefferson*, pp. 3, 6–7.

[7] *Ibid.*, p. 43.

[8] *Ibid.*, p. 54.

[9] *Ibid.*, p. 59.

[10] *Ibid.*, p. 45.

[11] *Ibid.*, p. 36.

[12] *Ibid.*, pp. 130, 132, 133.

[13] *Ibid.*, p. 125.

[14] *Ibid.*, pp. 171, 185, 187.

[15] *Ibid.*, pp. 195–196.

[16] *Ibid.*, p. xi.

[17] *Ibid.*, pp. 247, 248.

[18] *Ibid.*, p. 226.

[19] *Ibid.*, pp. 237–238.

[20] Boorstin, *The Genius of American Politics* (Chicago: University of Chicago Press, 1953).

[21] *Ibid.*, p. 6.

[22] *Ibid.*, p. 27.

[23] *Ibid.*, p. 98.

[24] *Ibid.*, p. 141.

[25] *Ibid.*, pp. 167–168.

[26] *Ibid.*, p. 174.

[27] *Ibid.*, pp. 172–173, 179–180.

[28] *Ibid.*, p. 184.

[29] *Ibid.*, p. 189.

[30] Boorstin, *The Americans: The Colonial Experience* (New York: Random House, 1958), p. 1.

[31] *Ibid.*, p. 64.

[32] *Ibid.*, pp. 150, 159.

[33] *Ibid.*, p. 158.

[34] Boorstin, *The Image* (New York: Atheneum, 1962), p. 31.

[35] *Ibid.*, p. 6.

[36] *Ibid.*, p. 119.

[37] *Ibid.*, pp. 121, 212.

[38] *Ibid.*, p. 201.

[39] Boorstin, *The Genius of American Politics*, p. 170.

[40] Boorstin, *The Image*, pp. 240ff.

Index

INDEX